SPENDI

How To Books on Living & Working Abroad

Applying for a United States Visa
Backpacking Round Europe
Become an Au Pair
Doing Voluntary Work Abroad
Emigrate
Finding a Job in Canada
Finding Work Overseas
Find Temporary Work Abroad
Get a Job Abroad
Get a Job in America
Get a Job in Australia
Get a Job in Europe
Get a Job in France
Get a Job in Germany
Get a Job in Hotels & Catering
Get a Job in Travel & Tourism
Live & Work in America
Live & Work in Australia
Live & Work in France
Live & Work in Germany
Live & Work in the Gulf
Live & Work in Italy
Live & Work in Japan
Live & Work in New Zealand
Live & Work in Portugal

Living & Working in Britain
Living & Working in Canada
Living & Working in China
Living & Working in Hong Kong
Living & Working in Saudi Arabia
Living & Working in the Netherlands
Master Languages
Obtaining Visas & Work Permits
Rent & Buy Property in France
Rent & Buy Property in Italy
Retire Abroad
Selling into Japan
Setting Up Home in Florida
Spending a Year Abroad
Study Abroad
Teach Abroad
Travel Round the World
Working Abroad
Working as a Holiday Rep
Working in Japan
Working in the Gulf
Working on Contract Worldwide
Working on Cruise Ships
Your Own Business in Europe

Other titles in preparation

The How To series now contains more than 200 titles in the following categories:

Business Basics
Family Reference
Jobs & Careers
Living & Working Abroad
Student Handbooks
Successful Writing

Please send for a free copy of the latest catalogue for full details
(see back cover for address).

LIVING & WORKING ABROAD

SPENDING A YEAR ABROAD

How to have the time of your
life anywhere around the world

Nick Vandome

3rd edition

IT'S THE ONLY WAY I COULD
GET HER TO COME!

How To Books

By the same author

How to Find Temporary Work Abroad
How to Get a Job in Australia
How to Travel Round the World

British Library Cataloguing-in-Publication data
A catalogue record for this book is available from the British Library.

Cartoons by Mike Flanagan

© 1997 by Nick Vandome

Published by How To Books Ltd, Plymbridge House, Estover Road,
Plymouth PL6 7PZ, United Kingdom.
Tel: (01752) 202301. Fax: (01752) 202331.

First published 1992
Second edition (revised and updated) 1995
Third edition 1997

Note: The material contained in this book is set out in good faith for general
guidance and no liability can be accepted for loss or expense incurred as a
result of relying in particular circumstances on statements made in the book.
The laws and regulations are complex and liable to change, and readers
should check the current position with the relevant authorities before making
personal arrangements.

Produced for How To Books by Deer Park Productions.
Typeset by Kestrel Data, Exeter
Printed and bound in Great Britain by The Cromwell Press, Broughton Gifford,
Melksham, Wiltshire.

Contents

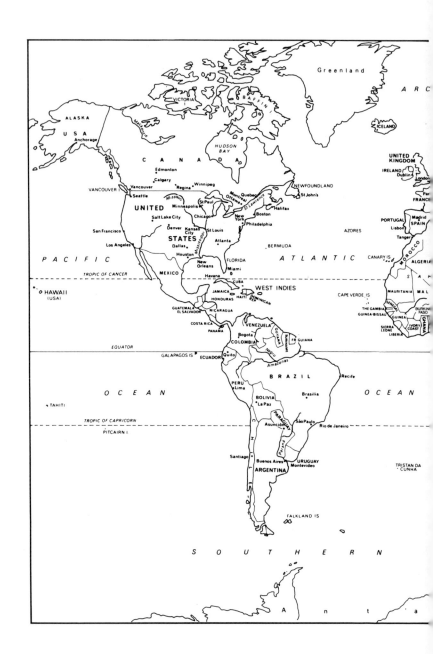

Preface

to Third Edition

School leavers, students, graduates, young married couples, middle-aged couples, accountants who have taken early retirement and a seventy-year-old grandmother. All of these people are very different and I have encountered them all during my time of travelling and writing about spending a year abroad. If they prove anything, it is that a year abroad is for *anyone*. There is no such thing as a typical year abroad and each experience is unique and memorable for the person involved.

Just as all kinds of people can undertake a year abroad, so there are numerous ways to spend a year (or indeed longer if so desired) in far-flung places. The options are as varied as the stamps in a traveller's passport: from teaching English in Nepal, to studying in Swaziland, to working in a youth camp in America, to a year of exotic travel. This book covers some of these options, but in addition to this, one golden rule should be followed: don't be afraid to use your initiative and do something different. (And if you do, let me know for the next edition!)

Whatever you do in your year abroad you not only have a great responsibility to yourself but you also have a responsibility to the places you visit. Never forget that you are a visitor and always treat people and places with respect.

A book of this type relies on the help, directly and indirectly, of a great many people. My thanks go to everyone who has helped fill in the gaps where my own experience was lacking, and in particular to the travellers who have written to me to offer advice and tell me about their experiences. I am always grateful for any comments, suggestions and additional information from anyone who has spent a year abroad. It is impossible for one person to cover everything, so all contributions will be gratefully received. Send them to the author, c/o How To Books Ltd, Plymbridge House, Estover Road, Plymouth PL6 7PZ.

If you have ever dreamed of spending a year abroad then hopefully this book can help bring the reality a bit closer.

Nick Vandome

1
Preparing Before You Go

In some ways the hardest part about planning a year abroad is the initial decision to take the plunge and pack your bags. However exciting it may seem there will always be doubts and apprehensions —leaving family and friends, foregoing stability and security for unknown places, and the thought that you may never see your pet goldfish again.

These doubts are perfectly normal and it would be more worrying if you did not occasionally have second thoughts. However, you have to weigh these up against the opportunities you will miss if you stay at home and resist the temptation to pack up and go. The doubts you have as you stare at the ceiling in the middle of the night rarely look as threatening in the light of day. Although a year abroad is a big step things will be remarkably similar when you return and, after a couple of weeks at home, you may be itching to leave again.

Despite this a year abroad is not for everyone and it is a decision that should be taken seriously and not in an offhand, whimsical fashion.

WHY DO IT?

Traditionally a year abroad is taken for three main reasons:

- A transitional year between school and university.
- To gain wider experience before entering the job market.
- An irresistible case of wanderlust.

After school
The first opportunity most people will have for a year abroad will be when they finish school. After years of calculus, homework and school dinners the prospect of time abroad is an exciting one.

However, it should be looked at as an opportunity for development and not just an excuse to escape from studying for a year.

Careers officers prefer pupils spending a year abroad between school and university to pursue a structured approach rather than a year of aimless wandering. Donald MacDonald, the careers master at George Watson's College in Edinburgh, takes a great interest in pupils who are contemplating a year abroad and in general he steers them away from the freelance approach: 'We tend to take the university line; that is we prefer pupils to do something constructive as opposed to a year in the Mediterranean with a guitar and a bed-roll'. This is good advice and it is worth remembering that you can undertake a second year abroad once you have completed any further education that you choose.

After university/college

A year abroad after university offers the most scope but it is also the stage at which eyebrows begin to be raised and questions such as 'Where will it all end?' are aired. The respectable world of employment views the concept of a year abroad with a certain amount of circumspection. They like it to have definite boundaries —with a specific end in sight. With this in mind several employers now offer deferred job opportunities. Through this you will be given a job before you graduate, but it will be deferred for a year so you can spend time overseas. This benefits both parties: you know you will have a job when you return, and the company knows they will have a more worldly-wise employee.

If you do not want the strictures of knowing that you *have* to come back after a year (a year abroad is an elastic creature that tends to expand rather than contract) then you should stick to your guns and worry about the consequences later. This may sound like irresponsible advice but your working career will occupy over 40 years of your life and if you have the confidence to spend a year abroad then you will have the ability to take up a career whenever you return. Also, a year abroad will probably provide more memorable moments than the rest of your entire working life.

Wanderlust

It would be naive to suggest that school leavers and graduates are the only people interested in spending a year abroad. For people of all ages, and from all walks of life, it is a realistic and viable option. Many people, who see the world as being more than their own town and their own country, spend a year abroad for the simple reason of experiencing different cultures and seeing how people on other parts of our planet live. If this applies to you then a year abroad should be a real possibility. A curious, inquisitive mind is one of the best reasons for leaving the rat-race behind and discovering the rest of the world.

WHY NOT DO IT?

Luckily, human nature being what it is, not everyone wants to do the same thing. For the traveller this is something of a relief— after all, someone has to stay here to keep the home fires burning—and there are some people who have no inclination or desire to spend a year abroad. However, there are others who warm to the abstract image but who would not fare too well with the nitty-gritty of the reality. This is when people have to seriously question their motives and ask if they are thinking of spending a year abroad for any of these reasons:

- romantic notions of adventure and excitement
- it seems like a 'good idea'
- someone else is doing it.

The romantic myth

A common response to people who have spent a year abroad is, 'That sounds so exciting and romantic . . . I wish I could do it!' Well yes, it does have its moments of excitement, adventure and romance. But it also consists of moments of home-sickness, physical sickness, uncertainties, and having to wash your dirty socks. It will not transform your personality—you will be living your life in a different environment but you will not be transformed into a different person.

If you think that all your domestic worries are going to disappear when you are abroad and you are going to be transported into some type of nirvana then it would be best to stay at home with a good travelbook. This is not meant to be harsh—if you undertake a year abroad under any kind of misconception then it is likely to be a very miserable experience.

A good idea at the time

If the thought of a year abroad comes to you in a bolt from the blue it is best to sit down and digest the idea for a while. Consider your motives, your ambitions and the effect it will have on your life. If you still think it is a good idea then go for it.

Peer pressure
We all succumb to peer pressure at some time in our lives, but as far as a year abroad is concerned it is not a good moment to start. When you are considering this option peer pressure can come into play in two ways. You may be won over to the idea when it had not previously entered your mind, or you may be persuaded to do the same thing as one of your friends.

Having the idea of a year abroad put into your head is no bad thing, and from these little acorns wonderful experiences have blossomed. However, you have to be convinced that you want to do it and that you are not agreeing simply for friendships' sake. Similarly, do not agree to do the same thing as someone else unless it is something that you want to do anyway. If you agree to something against your better judgment it will lead to broken friendships and acrimonious rows in far-off places.

DECIDING WHAT TO DO

There are numerous possibilities, most of which can be done in a variety of combinations:

* A year of travel—expensive, but immense fun.
* Organised work—with a camping company such as Canvas Holidays, or a work camp such as Camp America.
* Casual work—hospitality trade, fruit-picking, labouring, factory work.
* Voluntary work—Voluntary Services Overseas, GAP Activity Projects, Project Trust.
* An educational year abroad—United World Colleges, the university ERASMUS Scheme, language schools.
* Teaching English as a Foreign Language.
* Working on a kibbutz.
* Freelance work—writing, photography, busking.

All of these will be dealt with in greater detail in later chapters but the most important thing to remember is to do what you *want* to do, not what other people tell you to do. If you have always yearned to work on a prawn trawler in Australia or canoe up the Amazon, then do it.

FUNDING A YEAR OUT

Unfortunately, when it comes to a year abroad, money does make the world go around. As with most things that are worthwhile or enjoyable the folding stuff is of great importance. Regardless of whether or not you are planning to work during your time abroad it is essential to have a reasonable amount of money before you start. The sum will vary depending on the countries you intend to visit and we will discuss this more fully in later chapters. However, Murphy's Financial Law (what can cost you money, will cost you money) is a close companion of the traveller, so it is a good idea to work out how much money you think you will need and then double it.

Calculating how much money you require is one thing, but earning it is another. Short of picking those elusive score-draws on the pools, or a distant relative dying and leaving you a small fortune from a sheep farm in Australia, the only way around this is that unromantic notion of nose-to-the-grindstone, and save, save, save.

What are the options?
Several options can be considered:

Casual work
This can take the form of almost anything, as long as it brings in money. It could be bar work, packing biscuits in a factory, filling supermarket shelves, or working on a building site. Unfortunately, due to the low paid status of these types of jobs it may be necessary to have two jobs and you may find yourself working 60-70 hours a week. This can be mildly soul-destroying but, as you are putting yet another can on yet another shelf, remember the goal that you have in mind. And besides, it will be valuable experience for finding similar jobs abroad.

Professional work
If you have the qualifications it can be tempting to work in a vocational job in order to earn a higher salary before going abroad. However, unless you make your intentions very clear when you

begin, this is not advisable. When you come back from your year abroad you will have great difficulty convincing any employers that you are not going to do exactly the same again. One way around this is to take a sabbatical from work—but you will have to convince your firm that it will be beneficial to them to let you have a year off to indulge your peripatetic inclinations.

Company sponsorship
Occasionally newspapers carry stories about people who have been sponsored by a company to undertake a particular activity abroad. If you have a unique idea for your time overseas then this is a possible source of funds, but in these days of belt-tightening and economic recession it is increasingly difficult to convince companies to part with their cash for your benefit. If you do try this approach it is important to stress the advantages that you would bring to the company.

Loan
A bank loan to help fund a year abroad is a possibility but it would undoubtedly cause more problems than it would solve. A simpler idea for ready finance is the traveller's invaluable companion, the credit card (see Chapter 11, p. 154).

Sacrifices
The period before you leave for your year abroad can be difficult and, at times, depressing. You will be working hard and at the same time trying to save as much money as possible. You will probably not be able to afford any luxuries for yourself and your friends may think that you are becoming a workaholic recluse. But these sacrifices need to be made and you will soon forget about the difficult times when you are heading overseas.

As far as money is concerned, set yourself a specific target and make sure you keep to it. Whether you achieve your goal will be a good indication of how serious you are about the whole venture.

CHECKLIST

1. Are you sure of your ambitions?
2. Have you looked at all the options?
3. Have you taken independent advice?
4. Are you being pressured to do something against your wishes?

5. Will you have adequate finances?
6. Have you set a specific date for your departure, and are you working towards it?

CHECK YOUR YEAR OUT SUITABILITY

1. A friend tells you that she is going to spend a year canoeing up the Amazon. Do you:
a Immediately dive into your jungle gear and turn up on her doorstep?
b Sit dreaming of lost cities and undiscovered tribes?
c Research other possibilities for spending a year in South America?

2. You are busy saving for a year abroad. Your friends arrive at your house and invite you to the pub. Do you:
a Go for half an hour and sit unhappily drinking soda water?
b Go to the pub, drink a week's savings and then tell your friends about all the amazing things you are going to do?
c Decline the invitation and console yourself with the thought of what you are going to be doing in the near future?

3. While saving for a year abroad you are surrounded by people with large sums of money. Do you feel:
a Smug?
b Resentful?
c Dedicated?

4. People keep telling you that you are doing the wrong thing. Do you:
a Break down in tears?
b Punch someone on the nose?
c Smile contentedly?

5. Your bank manager keeps telling you that you are doing the wrong thing. Do you:
a Change banks?
b Punch him on the nose?
c Save harder?

6. A friend tells you of all the diseases you could catch while abroad. Do you:

a Begin imagining your agonising death in a far-off land?

b Say that you have never been sick in your life?

c Go to your doctor for reassurance?

7. A civil war breaks out in one of the countries you intend to visit. Do you:

a Change your destination immediately?

b Arm yourself with a Kalashnikov and a rocket launcher?

c Contact the Foreign Office to see what the situation is?

Your score

Mostly a. You have the potential for a year abroad but you have to think seriously about the implications and practicalities of the situation.

Mostly b. A year abroad would be a disaster and you would probably get yourself killed in the first week. You like the image of distant lands and excitement but you should stick to documentaries on the TV.

Mostly c. You have a good grasp of what a year abroad will be like and you are prepared to make the necessary sacrifices. The basis for a very successful year.

2
Deciding When To Go

GOING BETWEEN SCHOOL AND UNIVERSITY

What's the official view?

Naturally enough, careers officers in schools want to see pupils benefit as much as possible from a year abroad. For this reason they generally recommend an organised project rather than a year 'bumming around' the world.

They also like to remind pupils that although it is a break from studying, if they are going on to further education they should not lose their academic instincts. Shewan Duthie, careers master at Robert Gordon College in Aberdeen, recognises the advantages in terms of personal and social development, but he is wary of its effects in an academic criteria: 'The main problem with a year abroad is that it has to be carefully planned to be worthwhile. All too often I have seen it used simply as a means of getting a break from the academic grind and, in the process, the pupils concerned have broken good study routines.'

In general, careers teachers have two pieces of advice:

● Think carefully about what you want to do.
● Be constructive.

What do the pupils think?

Due to an increased awareness of the benefits of a year abroad, school leavers are confronted with a variety of alternatives for a structured year, as Clare Bond from George Watson's College in Edinburgh explains:

'I was very surprised by the number of schemes and organisations there are to help fill gap years, and I feel sure that the trend towards deferred entry will continue because as the number of options grow there will be something for everyone. Having examined the numerous options available, from getting a job to working with Tibetan refugees in Northern India, I have now settled on two choices.

'I will either be going to an American college to study, although this depends on the scholarship, or I will spend four months in Svalbard, 500 miles from the North Pole, on an expedition.'

Simon Peltenburg, one of Clare's classmates, is equally aware of the possibilities and sees some of the problems he will have to overcome:

'I intend to go off on a project such as GAP or Project Trust, as these allow me to go away for a whole year. This type of project seems to be a good option for a year abroad because a lot of the organisation is already done, and there is also a certain amount of help and back-up.

'The main problem I have encountered so far is the fact that some teachers and organisations are sceptical of a year abroad. I feel its reputation can be muddied by people who are naive and lazy, but everyone I know spending a year abroad would much rather be active than inert.'

Friends' reactions

Clare has encountered mixed reactions to her proposed exploits:

'Interestingly enough opinion is divided among my friends. There are some who think that the prestige and the subsequent success of the scholarship candidates in the past make it the most attractive option. Others think that the unique opportunity to go to the Arctic and lead a totally different life for four months is so exciting I would be crazy not to go.

'My parents, although supportive, find it all a bit daunting and just tell me to think about it. There are also a small minority who shudder at the cost of it all and are glad to be going straight to university. A year out will be expensive but it is nevertheless a decision I am very glad I made.'

Looking at these views it is clear that school leavers contemplating a year abroad will have to address a number of questions:

1. Am I prepared to go to university a year later than most of my friends?
2. Can I raise the money and make the necessary financial sacrifices for a year abroad?
3. Do I want to undertake a single project for the whole year, or do two or three for a few months each?
4. Have I chosen something that will show I put my year abroad to good use?
5. Do I have alternatives if I am unable to do my first choice?

OPPORTUNITIES FOR SCHOOL LEAVERS

There is no reason why school leavers should not do some of the options mentioned in later chapters, but there are a few organisations who offer a year abroad specifically for this group.

Doing voluntary work

Undertaking voluntary work during a year abroad is an area that can be both challenging and fulfilling. The idea of helping humanity in exotic locations is an appealing one to many people but it is not a decision to be taken lightly. Before you consider applying to organisations involved in voluntary work overseas ask yourself a few questions to ascertain whether it is really for you:

1. Do you like working with people?
2. Can you adapt to new situations and environments?
3. Are you prepared to make sacrifices in terms of your own physical, financial and emotional well-being?
4. Do you know the realities involved in the type of voluntary work you are considering?
5. Are you prepared to 'rough it' if necessary?

If the answers are 'yes' then read on. There are two main options and in both cases you will have to pay some of the expense involved in getting you to your destination and getting you established. It is also worth remembering that voluntary work is not all smiling children and grateful villagers. There will be times when you wonder why you have made this choice, but it is one of the most rewarding options during a year abroad and something that will bring out personal characteristics that you thought were either well hidden or non-existent.

The organisations
GAP Activity Projects
  GAP House
  44 Queen's Road
  Reading
  Berkshire RG1 4BB
  Tel: (0118) 959 4914
Tailored specifically for school leavers for the year before they
go to university, GAP organises voluntary work experience in
34 countries, covering every continent. The selected volunteers
work in a variety of jobs including: helping the handicapped,
English language teaching, conservation work and office work. The
assignments range from three months to a year but they all finish
by the start of the next academic year. Interested pupils are
recommended to apply during the first term of their final school
year. Applicants must be 18 by the date they take up their
attachment.

Since GAP is an educational charity the successful applicants
have to pay certain costs. These include a registration fee (£30),
return air fare to your destination, a GAP fee that helps fund your
project (£440 in 1996), insurance and, in relevant cases, a Teaching
English as a Foreign Language course (approximately £200). This
may seem like a lot of money, particularly if you want to go to a
long-haul destination such as Australia. However, for this you will
have the services of an established organisation with a proven
reputation. As a first experience of an extended period abroad it
is to be recommended.

GAP is highly thought of by both universities and employers—
they like to see that time abroad is being spent constructively and
that there are prescribed time limits. GAP has recently initiated a
Business Partnership Scheme, whereby GAP volunteers are intro-
duced to various business groups. Obviously this benefits all parties
involved.

Other benefits come from the time spent abroad, as one group
of volunteers in Mexico explained:

'Work started the day after we arrived, as the building of the school
must be finished before term starts next Monday, so this involves
forming a chain—teacher, children, mothers, EVERYBODY—and
passing bricks from one pile to another. There is no denying that the
work is tiring, especially in the Mexican sun, but on the other hand it

is good to be part of such a determined community. The smiles and enthusiasm of the kids are really warming to see.'

Project Trust
   The Hebridean Centre
   Isle of Coll
   Argyll PA78 6TE
   Tel: (01879) 230 444
Provides opportunities for young people between 17 and 19 to serve overseas for a year. The type of work that is undertaken includes teaching, working in children's homes and hospitals, and outdoor work in countries in Africa, South America, Asia and the Middle East. Volunteers are housed by the host organisation and are paid a living allowance.

Students must be in full-time education at the time of applying and studying for qualifications acceptable for university entrance. As with GAP they need to raise a significant part of the cost involved; in 1996 this was approximately £3,000. Fundraising advice is given to help successful applicants raise this sum.

Applications open in March and selection courses take place from October to January the following year. Applicants are usually interviewed in their own area and the successful ones will then take part in a four-day selection course on the Isle of Coll. Of these, 80 per cent are offered places overseas.

Youth Exchange Centre
   10 Spring Gardens
   London SW1A 2BN
   Tel: (0171) 389 4030
Works on community programmes in Germany and offers volunteers the chance to work for up to six months. Particularly active with the disadvantaged.

Concordia (Youth Service Volunteers)
   8 Brunswick Place
   Hove
   East Sussex BN3 1ET
   Tel: (01273) 772086
Organises international work camps during the summer. Applicants should be over 18 for camps in Europe. Accommodation is provided but not expenses.

Points to consider
- Can you raise the required amount of money?
- Are you prepared for such a challenge at this point in your life?
- What benefits will it bring you at the time?
- What benefits will it bring you after the event?

USING THE YEAR FOR EDUCATION

There are a number of opportunities in education, ranging from exchanges for a few weeks to the chance to study for two years at a school abroad.

United World Colleges (UWC)
  Lynton House
  Tavistock Square
  London WC1H 9LT
  Tel: (0171) 388 2066

An organisation which promotes peace through the international education of young people aged 16–18. They run ten colleges throughout the world: in Swaziland, Singapore, America, Canada, Hong Kong, Venezuela, Italy, Wales, Norway and India (opening in 1997). Each college follows the International Baccalaureate (IB) syllabus, which is taken over the same period as A levels but consists of the study of six subjects instead of three.

UWC schools are open to pupils regardless of race, colour, creed or ability to pay, as UWC will sponsor anyone who is chosen but cannot afford the fees. Applicants will not only be considered on their academic abilities but also on their personal qualities.

It is a unique opportunity to spend **two** years abroad studying for the IB qualification which will then give you access to universities around the world. Lucy Delap, a pupil from Dulwich, went to the Waterford Kamhlaba College in Swaziland and it extended both her social and educational horizons:

'There are students from 45 countries at Waterford and because of the variety everyone is open-minded and friendly. I felt at home after only one week. It also gives you a more balanced view of the world, not just the British one.'

Part of the IB programme involves community service and Lucy also found this a valuable experience while looking after children in a local hospital:

'It can be quite harrowing at times because of the lack of equipment and facilities, but in a way that makes you feel more useful. Doing community service in a Third World country you know you are helping people directly and not just being a spectator.'

People interested in UWC and the IB should approach them at the above address. The selection process is rigorous and is done by a selection committee in the applicants own country.

Other educational years abroad
If you want to organise an independent year abroad at a school overseas you should initially contact:

Central Bureau for Educational Visits and Exchanges (part of the British Council)
    10 Spring Gardens
    London SW1A 2BN
    Tel: (0171) 389 4004

                        or

    3 Bruntsfield Crescent
    Edinburgh EH10 4HD
    Tel: (0131) 447 8024

                        or

    1 Chlorine Gardens
    Belfast BT9 5DJ
    Tel: (01232) 664418/9
They will be able to give you practical advice about studying abroad and highlight some of the opportunities most applicable to your own situation. They publish a useful book on the subject, *Home from Home*.

Is it right for me?
Before you spend a year, or a term, at an overseas school you should discuss it with your parents and your careers teacher, and ask yourself some important questions:

1. How will I benefit from the experience?
2. Will it help or hinder my further education?
3. Will I need a language to study abroad?
4. How much will it cost—getting there, fees, accommodation, living expenses?
5. What type of curriculum will I be studying?
6. Do I want to study abroad for one term or a longer period?

Exchanges, homestays and termstays

An excellent way to learn a language and get to know a foreign country is to stay there with a family and attend classes at a local school. This can be done for anything from two weeks to ten months and there are schemes that cover the world. For further information contact:

Central Bureau for Educational Visits and Exchanges (see above).

Cultural and Educational Services Abroad (CESA)
    Western House, Malpas
    Truro
    Cornwall TR1 0SQ
    Tel: (01872) 225300
Sends students (from 13 to 79) on language courses worldwide. Languages including French, German, Spanish, Italian, Dutch, Japanese, Russian, Greek, Portuguese, Chinese, Arabic, Hebrew, Czech and Swedish.

Intercultural Educational Programme (IEP)
    33 Seymour Place
    London W1H 5AP
    Tel: (0171) 402 3305
Provides 16- to 18-year-olds with the chance to spend up to a year in countries as diverse as Thailand and Venezuela. Participants stay with local families and attend classes at school. The cost is approximately £3,300 but grants of up to £3,000 are available. Applicants need to be in full-time education.

International Educational Opportunities
    28 Canterbury Road
    Lydden

Dover
Kent CT15 7ER
Tel: (01304) 823631
Organises homestays and termstays in Europe and America.

Scholarships
Some schools run programmes with overseas universities, generally in America, where students can spend a year between school and a place at a British university. Consult your careers teacher to see if there is such a scheme available at your school.

Expeditions
The most realistic option for students wishing to undertake some form of expedition is:

Raleigh International
  27 Parsons Green Lane
  London SW6 4HS
  Tel: (0171) 371 8585
They operate scientific research and community projects in places including Australia and Zimbabwe. Applicants must be between 17 and 25 and they must raise a substantial amount of the £3,000 costs.

DURING AND AFTER UNIVERSITY

At this point the world is very much your proverbial oyster. The various options for general work and travel will be listed and discussed in the following chapters. However, there are some options that are particularly useful for students or graduates.

THE BRITISH UNIVERSITIES NORTH AMERICA CLUB (BUNAC)

BUNAC
  16 Bowling Green Lane
  London EC1R 0BD
  Tel: (0171) 251 3472

You can also join through your local campus club.

Since the early 1960s BUNAC has been known as an excellent outlet for an area that it notoriously difficult to penetrate— employment in North America. While this aspect of BUNAC is going from strength to strength they have added Australia, Jamaica and Malta to their repertoire. They also have a number of other strings to their bow (all prices were for 1996).

Bunacamp
A well established and popular programme which sends camp counsellors to children's summer camps in America and Canada. They offer formal instruction in sports, arts and crafts, drama, nature, computers and science. Anyone between 19½ and 35 is eligible to apply (students and non-students), but you must enjoy working with children and preferably have held a leadership role such as school prefect, youth leader, scout or guide. A qualification in sports, crafts or music may help you obtain a position as a specialist counsellor but this is by no means essential. The most important qualification is a positive personality and a keen participation in a relevant hobby or interest.

There are three types of camps: **agency camps,** which are general camps with scouts, guides and inner-city children; **specialist camps for handicapped children; specialist camps teaching one sport,** such as tennis. The counsellors work for approximately two months and they are then free to travel around America.

Interviews take place during the first and second terms of the university year and interested parties should get their applications in as soon as possible, as interviews are arranged on a first-come-first-served basis. Having said that, *all* first-time applicants are interviewed.

Successful applicants will have to pay a £59 registration fee (£67 in Ireland) and join BUNAC for £4 (£5). For camp counsellors proof of $400 in funds is required For this BUNAC will provide you with:

- Return airfare
- J-1 Work and Travel Visa
- Travel to and from your camp
- Your food and lodgings for the period you are at the camp
- A salary of $420 for under 21s and $480 for over 21s. This is

in total for your time at camp and includes deductions for your
airfare and suchlike.

One Bunacamper summed up the programme:

'The organisation makes everything easy and straightforward for someone going to America for the first time. It was possibly the hardest thing
I have ever done, but the most valuable. I learnt organisation, patience,
common sense and a lot about myself.'

KAMP (Kitchen and Maintenance Programme)

This is ideal for people who would like to work on a summer camp
but do not want to work directly with children. It is similar to
Bunacamp in that airfares and visas are arranged in advance but it
differs in that you can choose what type of work you want to do
(BUNAC has a directory of the various jobs). The choices available
include kitchen, dining room, cooking (some experience needed),
maintenance, porter, cleaning and driving.

Applicants must be members of BUNAC, be in full-time tertiary
education studying a degree course or an HND and be available
for work by June. The registration fee is £59 and during the time
you are on KAMP you will receive a total minimum salary of $570.
Proof of funds of $400 is required. You will be able to travel in
America for approximately six weeks after you leave.

Work America

One of the best ways to work in America—and one of the very few
that will allow you to legally do casual work in this country.

Any current, full-time student doing a tertiary or postgraduate
course at degree or HND level in England, Scotland or Wales
(students in Northern Ireland should apply through USIT) is
eligible. The programme provides students with a place on the
'Exchange Visitor Program' and the invaluable J-1 visa with which
you can then travel and work in any part of America. You can
either arrange a job before you go—BUNAC will aid you in this
with their free Job Directory—or you can be sponsored by an
American citizen. If you know someone in America who would be
prepared to do this it is the ideal situation because you can then
go your own way and find work as you go.

The registration fee for Work America is £81 and on top of this
you will need the cost of your flight (approximately £419) and

insurance (£89), both of which BUNAC will help organise for you, and proof of personal funds of up to $800 if you are going to look for work on your own. If you have a job arranged before you go you will need proof of funds of $400. Although this may seem like a large outlay compared with BUNACAMP or KAMP it is to be remembered that you will be working in a job with a realistic salary—the average weekly income on the programme is £190. All successful applicants are required to attend an orientation course in December.

Personal experience
Grant Cairncross took part in Work America and found his time in Boston very enlightening:

'Initially I was looking for work in the smarter Boston bars. However, I soon found that most of them wanted people with generations of experience and what amounted to a bartenders degree. I soon realised that I had to lower my sights a little. After knocking on a lot of doors and walking around most of Boston I eventually found a job in what must have been one of the roughest bars in town. There were fights most days and a popular activity was breaking pool cues over people's heads. I was even threatened with a gun on one occasion. Despite this, or maybe because of it, I had an incredible time—the locals were all very friendly to me, I earned a good wage and saw a side of life I would never have experienced at home. I would thoroughly recommend it.'

Work Canada
Similar to Work America but with two important differences:

1. You have to be returning to full-time tertiary education, which precludes final-year students but allows people who are taking a year off between school and university—providing they have an unconditional place at a university, polytechnic or college.
2. The scheme lasts for up to six months.

An ideal way to see a diverse country. The registration fee is £79. Proof of funds of $600 is required if you have a job arranged, and $1500 if you are going to look for work when you get there.

Work Australia
Open to any UK citizen between 18 and 25. Similar to making your own way on a Holiday Working Visa, but BUNAC offer help

with booking flights and arranging insurance, and an information service with their co-operators the Student Service Australia (SSA). Advice can be sought from them throughout your time Down Under. £2000 is required as proof of funds.

Work Jamaica

A relatively new and small programme which provides full-time students in Britain with the opportunity of working in Jamaica during the summer. Although it is a self-help programme like Work America and Work Canada it is not a self-financing operation and monetary gain is not its aim. People who have been on the programme relate that the experience gained is far greater than the contents of a pay packet.

The programme, which costs £915, includes flight, accommodation on arrival, orientation, work permission, support funds and insurance. There is also back-up support from the Jamaica Organisation of Youth and Student Tourists (JOYST). There is also a Teach Jamaica programme which costs £880 for a year, and £400 proof of funds is required.

New programmes

From 1997 there will be new programmes in Ghana, New Zealand, South Africa and Spain. Contact BUNAC for details.

CAMP AMERICA

Camp America
    American Institute for Foreign Study (UK) Ltd
    37A Queen's Gate
    London SW7 5HR
    Tel: (0171) 581 7373
Similar in many respects to BUNACAMP. Five main options are offered:

(Pocket money is for 1997 and is paid at the end of the programme).

1. *Camp counsellor.* Specialist or general. Pocket-money wages range from $220–$670, depending on age and experience.

2. *Campower.* As with KAMP and only available to students. Wages are $420–$520 for the nine-week period of the camp.

3. *Family companion*. This is a programme which places applicants with American families and he or she has responsibilities for helping to look after the host family's children. Applicants must be students aged 18–24, possess a full driving licence and preferably be non-smokers. Unfortunately, there is little demand for male family companions. Pocket money is $470 for a minimum 10 weeks.

4. *Infirmary assistant*. People with medical training are required to assist in the camp's medical facilities. Other duties permitting, the infirmary assistants are often asked to help in other areas of the camp. Pocket money is $520 for qualified infirmary assistants.

5. *Special needs*. People with experience of working with mentally or physically disabled people are required to work in special needs camps. The work can be very hard and demanding, but it is ultimately very rewarding.

A further option is also offered: the chance to spend a year in America on the **Au Pair in America** programme. If you are aged 18–25 you can get more information about this programme from:

Au Pair in America
   Dept. CA
   37 Queen's Gate
   London SW7 5HR
   Tel: (0171) 581 7322

Other work camp organisations
These include:

TocH
   1 Forest Close
   Wendover
   Aylesbury
   Bucks HP22 6BT
   Tel: (01296) 623911

YMCA International Camp Counsellor Programme
National Councils of YMCAs
640 Forest Road
London E17 3DZ
Tel: (0181) 520 5599

OPPORTUNITIES IN EDUCATION

Europe

*European Community Action Scheme for the Mobility of
University Students (ERASMUS)*
A scheme whereby students at British universities can spend a year
or a term at another EC university. This counts towards the final
degree, and although languages do usually form part of the courses
they are not all specifically for language students.

Individual universities will be able to pass on information about
their participation in the ERASMUS scheme and what courses are
on offer. For a full list contact:

ERASMUS Bureau
Rue d'Arlon 15
1040 Brussels
Belgium

Visiting studentships
Students with itchy feet can consider spending a year abroad as
visiting students. This will not count towards your degree in
Britain but you will attend lectures as an *auditeur*, ie not sitting
exams. You will also attend a special course of study for foreign
students.

If you are interested in being a visiting student for a year you
should apply personally to universities of your choice.

International universities
Schiller International University
51–55 Waterloo Road
London SE1 8TX
Tel: (0171) 928 8484

The International University
    1301 S Nolland Road
    Independence
    Missouri 64055
    USA

US International University
    10455 Pomerado Road
    San Diego
    California CA 92131
    USA

and

    The Avenue
    Bushey
    Herts WS2 2LN

Language Assistant Exchange Scheme

This is run by the Central Bureau for Educational Visits and Exchanges (see above) and the scheme sends students (usually language students) to work in schools and colleges in Europe and in some countries in Africa and South America.

Scholarships

Students wishing to gain scholarships to American universities should consult *Scholarships for International Students* available from:

Careers Research and Advisory Centre/Hobsons Ltd
    Bateman Street
    Cambridge CB2 1LZ
    Tel: (01223) 460 277

This lists 1,100 universities and colleges in the USA which offer various scholarships.

THE DRAWBACKS OF A YEAR ABROAD AFTER UNIVERSITY

Leaving behind the conventions

Although the number of people spending a year abroad after

university is increasing they are still in the minority. Some would say that this is reason enough to do it, while others may feel that they are becoming outcasts from the conveyor belt of school, further education, employment. But have the courage of your convictions and do not be afraid to buck the trend.

The comfort factor
While you are planning to embark on an impoverished existence abroad many of your university friends will be starting well-paid jobs. Or at least this is how it will seem. But in these days of rising graduate unemployment there are very few people who are guaranteed jobs once they leave university. Besides, in 40 years' time these same people may be complaining about their ulcer and wishing they had spent a year abroad when they had the chance. However, if you have a burning desire to own a Porsche with a matching car-phone, and eat business lunches of tofu and Perrier, then perhaps a year abroad is not for you.

Cupid's arrow
Many long-term romances have foundered when one partner has decided to spend a year abroad. This is an issue for the individuals themselves to discuss and come to terms with, and decide whether absence really does make the heart grow fonder. It is also worth noting that many marriages have been spawned by eyes meeting over a backpack in a far-off land.

A MID-LIFE YEAR ABROAD

It would be élitist, ageist and downright narrow-minded to suggest a year abroad should be confined to young people who have been through further education. Except for the organisations which have specific age restrictions, there is no reason why people taking a year abroad in mid-life should not do exactly the same as their younger counterparts. In some cases, such as various voluntary organisations, a more mature outlook can be a positive advantage.

After bringing up three children Marlene Douglas decided to indulge a long-held ambition to see the world. She reasoned that if she did not make the move now, while her grandchildren were still young, she might never realise her ambition. She soon discovered that age is a factor when you spend a year abroad in later life, as she was making her way across Canada:

'I learnt quickly that camping and travelling in a foreign land can be rewarding and character building, but since I will soon be 50 I foolishly thought I had a head start. There are limitations when you become my age and I learnt this early on—hitch-hiking and bussing it with a backpack takes its toll. While making my way towards North Bay I was trudging along barely able to raise a smile, far less my feet. At one point a goods train went rattling past only a few feet away and I was too tired even to be surprised.'

A month later Marlene found herself in Canmore, Alberta, where there is a strong Scottish community.

'I decided to stay long enough to buy a car and cruise down Route 66 instead of trudge. I worked as a chambermaid, and also sold water-colours of the local scenery. I was also present at the inaugural Canmore Highlands Games and I made a little extra cash by selling T-shirts with Gaelic motifs on them. It was during the Games that I came across the Canadian Marrow Dangling Contest—this one event alone made my time abroad worthwhile.'

Points to consider

● If you spend a year abroad you may still be young at heart but your physical state may not be as sprightly as it once was. Pace yourself and travel within your capabilities.

● Use your age to advantage. In most countries older people are respected and in some they are positively venerated. Accept this with good grace and enjoy the privilege.

● Although age may preclude you from many of the organised programmes for a year abroad you will probably be better qualified in several fields than younger people. Promote this when you are looking for work abroad—take a list of your qualifications and work experience and, if possible, some references. Don't be afraid to use your initiative—if you have brought up a family at home you may be able to pick up work as a nanny or a child-minder.

SUMMARY

1. If you are spending a year abroad after school you should consider doing it with an official organisation—their experience and contacts will ease your passage considerably.

2. Most organisations offer voluntary work or educational years abroad.

3. If you spend time abroad with an organisation such as BUNAC while you are at university or college you may have to return to full-time education. It might be worth looking into the possibility of taking a year off from your studies so you can spend a full year abroad.

4. Look into the opportunities for completing some of your degree at a foreign university.

5. A year abroad is for everyone—age is no drawback if you have the desire.

3
Undertaking Organised Work

TEACHING ENGLISH AS A FOREIGN LANGUAGE (TEFL)

From Japanese businessmen to Spanish schoolchildren, people around the globe want to learn English. This is good news for people wanting to work abroad and, with a little time, money and effort you can put yourself in a position where you are virtually guaranteed some form of job teaching English abroad. Initially you will have to ask yourself:

1. Do I want a recognised qualification?

2. Do I want to adopt the freelance approach?

The official line

In recent years there has been a marked increase in the number of organisations offering TEFL qualifications. These vary greatly in intensity, quality and price. The standard recognised qualification is the **Royal Society of Arts (RSA)/University of Cambridge Local Examinations Syndicate (UCLES) Certificate for Teaching English as a Foreign Language to Adults**. This is an intensive, practical course (four weeks if you undertake it on a full-time basis) and competition for places is stiff. You will have to attend an interview, at which you may be given a short written test dealing with common grammatical and semantic problems that may occur while you are teaching. With this in mind it would be a good idea to take a look at either *Rediscover Grammar* by D Crystal (Longman) or *Discover English* by R Bolitho and B Tomlinson (Heinemann).

How much will it cost?
Most RSA Certificate courses cost in the region of £700–£900. Although this is a large lump sum to pay out it is worth remembering that the Certificate is highly thought of around the world and once you have it you will be able to virtually pick a job in the country of your choosing. Look at it as a valuable investment.

Where can I do the course?
RSA Certificate courses are held at centres all over Britain. Four of the major ones are:

International House
  106 Piccadilly
  London W1V 9FL
  Tel: (0171) 491 2598

International Languages Centres Limited
  White Rock
  Hastings
  East Sussex TN34 1JY
  Tel: (01424) 720100
Sister centre of International House and they have a computerised database which matches applicants with TEFL qualifications to jobs primarily in the Middle or Far East.

Bell School of Languages
  1 Redcross Lane
  Cambridge CB2 2QX
  Tel: (01223) 247242
They run courses in Cambridge, Norwich, Saffron Walden, Bath and London.

Basil Paterson Tutorial College
  22 Abercromby Place
  Edinburgh EH3
  Tel: (0131) 556 7695
Runs a one month fulltime TEFL course for £850, or it can be undertaken as a six month part time course.

For a list of other centres offering RSA Certificates contact:

UCLES
  1 Hills Road
  Cambridge CB1 2EU

RSA
  8 John Adam Street
  London WC2N 8EY
  Tel: (0171) 930 5115

British Council
  The Information Centre
  Medlock Street
  Manchester M15 4AA
  Tel: (0161) 957 7755

You could also consult the EFL Directory, published by Summersdale.

Other qualifications
In addition to the RSA Certificate there are numerous other introductory TEFL courses around the country. Some of these have the advantage of being taught by organisations which have language schools abroad, so once you have gained your qualification you are very likely to be given a job with them.

Trinity College
  16 Park Crescent
  London W1N 4AP
Offer courses in Teaching Language to Speakers of Other Languages (TESOL) at their centres around the country. As intensive as the RSA Certificate but generally slightly cheaper. A well thought of alternative which allows you to teach children too.

Inlingua Cheltenham
  Rodney Lodge
  Rodney Road
  Cheltenham GL50 1JF
  Tel: (01242) 250493
Offer a variety or courses including a five week TESOL course for £725 and a two-week TEFL introduction course for £285.

Linguarama
  New Oxford House
  16 Waterloo Street
  Birmingham B2 5UG
  Tel: (0121) 632 9295

Courses in Alton, Bath, Birmingham, London, Manchester and Stratford-upon-Avon. Run a five-day introductory TEFL course for £205. Linguarama also run over 35 schools worldwide.

Primary House
    26 Cleeve Hill
    Bristol BS16 6HL
    Tel: (0117) 956 0496
Weekend courses for £250 and a home-study course for £180.

Surrey Language Centre
    Sandford House
    39 West Street
    Farnham
    Surrey GU9 7DR
    Tel: (01252) 723494
One week introductory TEFL course for £175. There is also a four week, full-time TESOL course for £650.

How do I get a job?
English as a Foreign Language (EFL) positions around the world are advertised in several publications, including the *Times Educational Supplement*, the *Education Guardian* (Tuesdays) and the *EFL Gazette* (Loop Format Limited, 10 Wright's Lane, London W8 6TA).

If you have a RSA Certificate and some TEFL experience (remember, there are numerous language schools in Britain at which you can teach before you go abroad), then you could apply to the British Council for a teaching job overseas. They are the largest international EFL employer and have 52 teaching centres around the world. Even with the above qualifications they may require a TEFL RSA Diploma, which can be undertaken after the Certificate and two years' teaching experience. For further information contact:

The British Council
    Information Centre
    Medlock Street
    Manchester M15 4AA
    Tel: (0161) 957 7755
    Fax: (0161) 957 7762

Other organisations who employ people with RSA Certificates and teaching experience include:

Bell Educational Trust
   Overseas Department
   The Lodge
   Redcross Lane
   Cambridge CB2 2QX

ILC Recruitment
   1 Riding House Street
   London W1A 3AS

English Worldwide
   17 New Concordia Wharf
   Mill Street
   London SE1 2BB

Advertised as 'the complete EFL recruitment service.' International House (as above), recruit for their 85 affiliated schools worldwide.

In some language schools abroad you will be asked to work long hours for only moderate wages. You may be given accommodation and you can supplement your salary with private teaching. If you put up a notice in the school or college you will invariably find a number of students who want to brush up on their subjunctives and polish their adverbial clauses.

Voluntary Service Overseas also employ people with TEFL qualifications. (See Voluntary Work).

Freelance
Not everyone likes to follow the official method and TEFL is an area where the one over-riding requirement is to be able to speak English. If you can do this, then with a little initiative and determination you will be able to find work abroad. If you have a degree, of any kind, or any similar qualifications, then it is a good idea to take the certificate with you. Prospective employers are sometimes just as impressed with this as a TEFL qualification.

Graeme Richardson, a New Zealander with an engineering degree but no TEFL qualification, has been teaching English in Japan for four years. He agrees that qualifications are important in some cases but stresses that confidence and a positive attitude are equally valuable.

'When I first arrived in Tokyo I studied the Monday edition of the *Japanese Times*, where there are hundreds of jobs advertised. After that it was just a case of going along to a language school and knocking on the door with my passport and a large dose of courage. Within a week I had two jobs and I have since worked in a high school and also taught numerous private students.

'There is a great demand for 'Native English Speakers' in Japan, and although it is getting more common to find people with TEFL qualifications there will always be the type of people who can sell snow to the Eskimos who will be able to find work here off their own back. The Japanese are very impressed by a business-like approach so you should dress well (invest in a reasonable suit) and present yourself in a positive, straight-forward fashion.'

As far as opportunity, pay and conditions are concerned Japan is one of the best places to work teaching English.

What can I expect?

Teaching conditions and pay vary dramatically from country to country but Graeme's summary of teaching in Japan covers most of the options available:

'You can bracket teaching conversational English in Japan into three groups. Firstly, there are the large language schools. They are located in all major centres and have a large staff and a steady turnover of employees. They sometimes advertise in the newspapers but the best bet is just to go knocking on a few doors. They have good working conditions and pay relatively well—more than language schools in other Asian and European countries.

'Secondly, there are positions in high schools and colleges. Working conditions are the same as for the Japanese teachers, and foreign teachers are treated very well by fellow staff. The pay is good but the jobs can be difficult to find. They are not usually advertised in the newspapers but if you have been teaching at a language school you may have contacts who will notify you of these jobs. A degree is very useful for jobs in schools and a TEFL qualification would give you an added advantage. The classes can be as many as 55 students.

'The final option is private conversation schools. These are backyard operations who cater mainly for housewives, children and students who want extra tuition. The working conditions are not the best and the pay is low. There are a few unscrupulous operators who run these schools and some of them go under and the teachers lose out. However, this means that people with no qualifications or experience can find work here quite easily. Most people use these schools as a stepping stone when they first arrive.'

Further reading
ELT Guide
  EFL Limited
  9 Hope Street
  Isle of Man 1MI 1AQ
A comprehensive directory of Introductory, Certificate, Diploma and MA courses. Also addresses for job-hunting overseas.

Teaching English Abroad, by Susan Griffith. From:
  Vacation Work
  9 Park End Street
  Oxford

How to Teach Abroad, by Roger Jones. From:
  How To Books
  Plymbridge House
  Estover Road
  Plymouth PL6 7PZ

Points to consider
1. You do not need a TEFL qualification to teach English abroad but it would definitely increase your chances of getting a good job.

2. If you only want to use teaching English as a stop-gap method for earning some extra money then adequate education qualifications may be enough for you to pick up some part-time teaching.

3. Be prepared for anything. Teaching English is not all grammar and spelling. You may find yourself singing nursery rhymes to four-year-olds in Zimbabwe or composing shopping lists for Japanese housewives. Flexibility and an active imagination will be your most valuable tools.

4. If you come across an employer who is unscrupulous with the students then you will probably be treated in the same fashion.

KIBBUTZ WORK

For people looking to immerse themselves in a different culture and spend time working abroad then Israel's kibbutzim must be considered.

A kibbutz (from the Hebrew word for group) is a voluntary, democratic community where people live and work together on a non-profit, non-competitive basis. Private property is limited to personal possessions.

There are currently over 270 kibbutzim in Israel, varying in size from 100 to 2,000 members. In total kibbutz members number 120,000, which represents approximately 2.8 per cent of Israel's population.

All kibbutzim have permanent members—kibbutzniks—but they all take on volunteer workers who live and work on the kibbutz for anything between five weeks and three months (although this can easily be extended). The kibbutzniks have their own living units but meals are taken together in the communal hall.

Points to consider before you go to a kibbutz as a volunteer worker

1. You must be in good physical and mental shape.
2. You will have to work long hours, six days a week, doing whatever jobs you are assigned. This could be working in the kitchens, picking melons or raising chickens.
3. You will be sleeping in cramped, spartan conditions.
4. You will have to conform to the rules and regulations of the kibbutz for the period you are living there.
5. Although you will be doing the same work as the kibbutzniks you will be treated like an outsider if you do not accept their way of life.

How do I apply to be a volunteer?
In Britain there is one organisation involved in sending volunteers to kibbutzim:

Kibbutz Representatives
  1A Accommodation Road
  London NW11 8EO
  Tel: (0181) 458 9235
  They make arrangements for three types of volunteers:

- **Working Visitor**—you are required to work for a certain amount of time and the rest of the day is your own. You must commit yourself for at least 8 weeks.
- **Working Hebrew**—in addition to your daily duties you have the opportunity to study Hebrew for 12 hours a week.
- **Ulpan**—designed mainly for people wishing to convert to the Jewish religion. Courses last for 5 months.

Volunteers have to be between 18 and 32 and those who are chosen will have to pay a fee of £50 and provide a medical report. Kibbutz Representatives will give you a letter of introduction to the kibbutz office in Tel Aviv, which gives you placement priority. You can also book your flight and insurance through them if you desire. A Kibbutz Package such as this costs approximately £312 in 1996.

Applying in Israel
In the past, most people who have made their own way to Israel and applied to kibbutzim through agencies in Tel Aviv agree that this is just as effective, and cheaper, than going through an agency in Britain. However, since the demand for kibbutzim volunteers can fluctuate from year to year it is a good idea to look at the merits of both methods.

If you should travel independently to Israel and apply on the spot then you should go to the principal kibbutzim agency in Tel Aviv. This is in effect a recruitment centre for the kibbutzim:

Kibbutz Program Center
  Volunteer Department
  Hayarkon Street 124
  (POB 3167)
  Tel Aviv 63573
  Tel: 03-221325/5246156

(Registration fee $50. You will also need your passport, medical certificate and insurance policy.)

If you do not want to do this then you can approach the kibbutzim directly. This is a bit hit and miss but several travellers have reported being given places in this fashion. For both methods you will need to have the relevant working papers with you—currently a B-4 'volunteer' visa.

The volunteer's tale
A volunteer at the Kibbutz Ramat Hakovesh comments:

'After working as a night shift worker in the factory making chicken pluckers I was put in the dining room, which was the pits. There was a lot of hanging around with nothing to do until everyone had finished and then I had to clean up. Then came a day in the avocado orchards, spraying weedkiller on the unwanted plants, and another day picking potatoes. Then it was into the kitchens, helping to prepare and cook all the food. I remained here until I left the kibbutz. Lucky because it was my favourite job of all, with plenty of variety.

'The kibbutzniks eat, shop and socialise together all the time. This creates a lot of gossiping and back-stabbing as everyone knows everyone else's business. Some of them also treat the volunteers like lowlife, despite the fact that whenever numbers started to fall they screamed that they could not manage without us. The younger generation, however, enjoy meeting people of similar ages from other parts of the world and generally like having volunteers around.'

What are the pros?
● learning about one society in depth
● meeting people from around the world
● working in a team
● opportunity for further travel once you leave the kibbutz.

And the cons?
● hard work
● unpaid—volunteers receive pocket money of approximately £25 a month
● occasional resentment from the kibbutzniks.

MOSHAVIM

These are similar to kibbutzim in concept but they differ in that the members can own their own machinery and houses. The work can be harder than on a kibbutz but in return the worker receives a basic wage for his efforts—approximately £200 a month. There is also more opportunity to mix with people outside the moshav.

Moshavim can be approached in a similar way to kibbutzim once you are in Israel. Alternatively, you could apply through:

Project 67 Ltd
  10 Hatton Gardens
  London EC1N 8AH
   Tel: (0171) 831 7626

Arrange placements for volunteers aged 21–35.

CAMPING FIRMS

A boom business in the last 15 years has been providing camping holidays in Europe for people who do not want the hassle of carrying their own tent and equipment. This has also been a godsend for people who want to work overseas—thousands of workers are taken on every year, either as on-site couriers or the muscle to put up and take down the tents.

The companies

- Canvas Holidays, 12 Abbey Park Road, Dunfermline, Fife KY12 7PD. Tel: (01383) 621000. Operate in Austria, France, Germany, Italy, Spain and Switzerland.

- Club Cantabrica Holidays Ltd, 146/148 London Road, St Albans, Hertfordshire AL1 1PQ. Tel: (01727) 833141. France, Greece, Italy and Spain.

- Club Med, 106/110 Brompton Road, London SW3 1JJ. Holiday villages in Europe and North Africa.

- Eurocamp PLC, Canute Court, Toft Road, Knutsford, Cheshire WA16 0NL. Tel: (01565) 755363. Austria, Belgium, France, Germany, Italy, Netherlands, Spain and Switzerland. (For summer jobs apply to: Overseas Recruitment Dept. (Ref. WH), Knutsford. Tel: (01565) 625522).

- PGL Ski Europe, Personnel Dept., Alton Court, Penyard Lane (878), Ross-on-Wye, Herefordshire HR9 5NR. Tel: (01989) 768168. France, Italy and Switzerland.

- PGL Young Adventures Ltd (address as above). Tel: (01989) 767833. Adventure holidays for young people in France.

- Ski Bound/Travelbound, Oliver House, 18 Marine Parade, Brighton, East Sussex BN2 1TL. Tel: (01273) 677777. Austria, France, Germany, Italy and also a schools option called Project Europe.

- Solaire Holidays, 1158 Stratford Road, Hall Green, Birmingham B28 8AF. Tel: (0121) 778 5061. France and Spain.

- Thomson Holidays, Overseas Personnel Department, Greater London House, Hampstead Road, London NW1 7SD. Tel: (0171) 387 9321. Require reps for their European and world-wide holiday resorts.

The jobs

Courier

Each company has at least one courier at each of its sites. Their job is to welcome the new arrivals, make sure their tent is clean and tidy and answer any queries they have. This may sound simple but the couriers usually end up being a cross between childminder, games organiser, tourist information officer, social organiser and crisis manager. Needless to say there is never a dull moment.

Couriers need to have a knowledge of the language of the country in which they hope to work, because they will have to liaise with the campsite owners and the locals.

Companies generally employ students but they are now branching out and employing a greater number of older people, including retired couples. The jobs last for approximately three months during the summer and the wages can be anything from £220 to £480 a month, with free accommodation. Most posts are filled by January but there is a high drop-out rate so if you are on a waiting list it may be worthwhile getting in touch with the company at fairly regular intervals.

Flying squad members/drivers

A more mobile job than couriers, as these are the people who travel around to all the campsites and put up and dismantle the tents. This usually takes place during March/April and September although some of the flying squad members and drivers are kept on for the whole summer as troubleshooters. No knowledge of a foreign language is required but the applicants should be fit, enthusiastic and possess a good sense of humour. Drivers usually need to be over 23 for insurance purposes.

ADVENTURE TRAVEL COMPANIES

An increasingly frequent sight on the overland routes through Africa and Asia are converted Bedford trucks taking travellers on overland tours. These are not only a good way to see the countries involved but the companies also employ drivers, cooks and mechanics. Sometimes the job will involve doing all three, in which case you will need either a Heavy Goods Vehicle Licence (HGV) or Passenger Service Vehicle Licence (PSV). Competition for these places is fierce and many of them are given to experienced people.

What will the work entail?
- Long hours
- Mechanical knowledge required
- Low pay but travel formalities are taken care of
- Essential to get on with people in claustrophobic conditions
- Stamina and endurance a must.

The companies

Guerba Expeditions (TF)
  40 Station Road
  Westbury
  Wiltshire BA13 3JN
  Tel: (01373) 826611

Exodus Travel
  9 Weir Road
  Balham
  London SW12 0LT
  Tel: (0181) 675 5550

Kumuka Expeditions
  40 Earls Court Road

Encounter Overland
  267 Old Brompton Road
  London SW5 9JA
  Tel: (0171) 370 6845

Dragoman Adventure Travel
  27 Camp Green
  Kenton Road
  Debenham
  Stowmarket
  Suffolk IP14 6LA
  Tel: (0171) 370 1930

Top Deck Travel
  131–135 Earls Court Road

London W8 6EJ
Tel: (0171) 937 8855

London SW5 9RH
Tel: (0171) 244 8641

The Imaginative Traveller
14 Barley Mow Passage
Chiswick
London W4 4PH
Tel: (0181) 742 3049

Journey Latin America
14–16 Devonshire Road
Chiswick
London W4 2HD
Tel: (0181) 747 8315

AU PAIR

Rightly or wrongly, this is one area that is almost exclusively reserved for women. In return for looking after a family's child/children you will receive your board and lodging and a wage that may not be much more than pocket money. Au pairs can work in Europe if they have a language, and it is one area where it is still possible to find a job in America or Canada; the social prestige of a British nanny is still common and even if you do not have any specific qualifications you could still find a job if you can exhibit a liking for hard work and a certain level of responsibility. Camp America runs a programme specifically for au pairs:

Au Pairs in America
Department CA
37 Queen's Gate
London SW7 5HR
Tel: (0171) 581 7322

Finding a job

If you are looking for an au pair position you could try approaching the numerous agencies which specialise in sending au pairs overseas. Most agencies charge a placement fee of approximately £40. They include:

Academy Au Pair Agency
42 Cedarhurst Drive
Eltham
London SE9 5PL
Tel: (0181) 294 1191

The Au Pair Agency
231 Hale Lane
Edgware
Middlesex HA8 9QF
Tel: (0181) 958 1750

Langtrain International
  Torquay Road
  Foxrock
  Dublin 18
  Tel: (3531) 2893876

Student Abroad
  11 Milton View
  Hitchin
  Herts SG4 0QD
  Tel: (01462) 438909

Problems Unlimited Agency
  86 Alexandra Road
  Windsor
  Berkshire SL4 1HU
  Tel: (01753) 830101

For a complete list of agencies, contact:

The Federation of Recruitment and Employment Services
  36–38 Mortimer Street
  London W1N 7RB
  Tel: (0171) 323 4300
Send a stamped, self-addressed envelope.

If you want to find an au pair placement yourself then you should consult *The Lady* magazine. This has a whole section of classified advertisements covering au pair work abroad. You can either contact some of the people who are advertising or, alternatively, put in your own notice offering your services.

What can I expect?

Since au pairs live with the families for whom they are working there can be friction over hours of employment and days off. It can be particularly difficult when an au pair is living with children who do not know the difference between work time and time off—they think you are there for their constant use. Before you take an au pair job you should find out:

● how many hours a day and a week you will be expected to work
● how many days off you will be given
● how many children you will have to look after
● if you are expected to cook and, if so, to what standard
● what other household chores will be expected of you
● how much you will be paid and whether you will receive more for extra duties such as babysitting.

For comprehensive coverage of au pairing consult: *The Au Pair and Nanny's Guide to Working Abroad*, Susan Griffith and Sharon Legg (Vacation Work), and *How to Become an Au Pair* by Mark Hempshell (How To Books, 1995).

WHAT TYPE OF WORK DO YOU WANT?

Ask yourself:
- Are you looking for money or adventure?
- Are you qualified for the areas for which you are applying?
- Do you have any paperwork that is required?
- Do you want a short-term position or something for the whole year?
- Do you want to travel while working or stay in one place?
- Do you want to do manual work or something using your mind?

VOLUNTARY WORK

Voluntary Service Overseas (VSO)
317 Putney Bridge Road
London SW15 2PN
Tel: (0181) 780 2266/1331

An option for people who are prepared to make a long-term commitment to voluntary work—the minimum tour of service is two years.

VSO is a charity organisation that sends people to help communities around the world. It covers a wide range of activities and is dedicated to improving the long-term development of areas in over 50 countries. It responds to specific needs by sending skilled workers including teacher trainers, midwives and experienced builders to countries where these skills can be put to practical use.

Each year 5,500 people apply to VSO, for approximately 700–800 posts. Candidates should ideally have a qualification or skill and also adaptability, resourcefulness and a good sense of humour. The successful applicants are then assigned postings in countries ranging from Laos to Belize. Great care is taken to send the right people to the most relevant area for their skills.

Since VSO requires a commitment of two years it is an option that has to be considered very carefully. It is not something for school-leavers but is ideal for a graduate or a skilled worker who is dedicated to voluntary work. Although volunteers do not receive a salary they are usually paid local wages and given local-standard accommodation. VSO grants are also paid before, during and after your time abroad.

One volunteer, Celia Marshall, is in no doubt as to the value of VSO:

> 'You'll often hear returned volunteers saying that they gained more than they gave when they went overseas. After three years as a volunteer in Ghana, I definitely fall into that category. I went to "share" my skills, as the VSO motto says, but I returned to Britain a good deal wiser about the meaning of sharing.'

Celia has since put that wisdom to good use, working for the Southern Voices Project in Manchester, promoting educational development through the acceptance of different cultures.

Several other organisations run workcamps abroad and it is sometimes necessary to gain experience in Europe or the UK before you will be sent to a Third World country. In most cases you will have to pay your own travel expenses, but food and accommodation are usually provided once you get to your destination.

International Voluntary Service (IVS)
  Old Hall, East Bergholt
  Colchester, Essex CO7 6TQ
  Tel: (01206) 298215
Concerned largely with arranging short-term placements in work-camps. Work in Europe, north and west Africa and the USA.

Skillshare Africa
  3 Belvoir Street
  Leicester LE1 6SL
  Tel: (01162) 541862
Opportunities for qualified and experienced staff to work in southern Africa for a minimum of two years.

United Nations Volunteers
  Palais des Nations
  1211 Geneva 10
  Switzerland
  Tel: (+41 22) 788 2455

Qualified and experienced volunteers from all UN countries needed for overseas service. Minimum of two years.

Health Projects Abroad
   PO Box 24
   Bakewell
   Derbyshire DE45 1ZW
   Tel: (01629) 640 053
Requires volunteers aged 18 to 28 with building skills and a liking for hard work. The volunteers will be working on four-month projects in Tanzania and elsewhere. Need to contribute £2000.

CIT
   78 Broud Street
   Nottingham NG1 3AJ
Projects in South America and Nicaragua for 3–6 months.

British Executive Service Overseas
   164 Vauxhall Bridge Road
   London SW1V 2RB
   Tel: (0171) 630 0644
Uses experienced, retired applicants to provide advice to projects overseas needing technical, financial and managerial help. Placements are usually for two to three months. Expenses are paid plus a small allowance.

Tear Fund
   100 Church Road
   Teddington
   Middlesex TW11 8QE
   Tel: (0181) 977 9144
Uses committed Christians on summer projects in Israel, Morocco and Sudan. Also co-ordinates with missionary bodies on assignments from two to four years. Applicants must possess a clean driving licence.

Christians Abroad
   1 Stockwell Green
   London SW9 9HP
   Tel: (0171) 737 7811
Places qualified workers abroad for two years.

East European Partnership (EEP)
  Carlton House
  27a Carlton Drive
  London SW15 2BZ
  Tel: (0181) 780 2841
A special unit of VSO which sends English teachers to Poland, the
Czech Republic, Bulgaria and Hungary for two years.

Richmond Fellowship International
  The Coach House
  8 Addison Road
  London W14 8DL
  Tel: (0171) 603 6373
The largest international voluntary organisation involved with
community mental health. Volunteers must be over 22. Operate in
the United States and some eastern European and developing
countries.

Health Unlimited
  3 Samford Street
  London SE1 9NT
  Tel: (0171) 928 8105
Recruit health care professionals for one year placements in primary
health care.
  For a fully comprehensive list of voluntary organisations consult:

International Directory of Voluntary Work (Vacation Work).
Volunteer Work (Central Bureau for Educational Visits and Ex-
  changes).
Doing Voluntary Work Abroad (How To Books).

Points to consider when applying for voluntary work
● What type of work will you be doing?
● Where will you be working?
● Will you be staying in one place or moving around?
● For how long will you need to commit yourself?
● How much will it cost?
● Some voluntary organisations have strong religious beliefs and
  you should share these if you are applying to them.

4
Finding Casual Work

For anyone spending a year abroad travelling it is likely that the concept of casual work will figure near the top of their agenda. Not only is it a way to earn some money for the next stage of your trip, it is also one of the best ways to meet people and get to know your surroundings properly. Even if you are in the enviable situation of having enough money to fund your trip you should still give some thought to picking up casual employment as you go—working can be an invaluable introduction to an area.

WHAT ARE THE OPPORTUNITIES?

Working in tourism
Wherever there are tourists there will be employment openings. There are a variety of opportunities within the general heading of tourism:

- hotels
- restaurants
- pubs
- nightclubs
- ski resorts.

The most likely places to find a job in tourism are Europe and Australia. There are numerous openings in North America but since work permits are so scarce for this part of the world you will almost certainly need to work illegally. This *is* done by large numbers of people every year but if you are caught you will be put on the next plane home and your chances of a return visit are slim.

How do I find a job?

If you are looking for a job in tourism in Europe it will help
enormously if you have at least one European language. For manual
jobs such as porters or dishwashers this may not be essential but
for more skilled jobs such as chefs and waiters you will not get
very far if you cannot speak the language of the country in which
you are seeking employment. Applications can be done in two
ways:

1. Applying before you go.
2. Knocking on doors when you arrive.

If you want to try and arrange a job before you go you should
invest in a copy of *The Directory of Summer Jobs Abroad* (Vacation Work). This lists hundreds of hotel and restaurant addresses throughout Europe. Pick the ones that sound most suited
to your needs and write to them (in their own language) and enclose
a self-addressed envelope and a couple of International Reply
Coupons, which can be bought at the Post Office.

When applying in this way it is important to sell yourself: there
are numerous skilled waiters and chefs in Europe so it would be
highly advantageous if you have experience and/or a catering
qualification.

This method of application is best for people who want to work
in larger hotels, restaurants and ski resorts (as chalet staff or
instructors). If you are interested in bar or nightclub work then
the 'being-in-the-right-place-at-the-right-time' method is best.
This is also necessary for similar work in Australia. Since this area
of the employment market tends to be extremely fluid, opportunism is sometimes more important than experience.

Try nightclubs and pubs in the morning (but not too early!)
since the manager may have more time to see you then. Even if
you are applying on spec make sure you are smart and respectable.
Treat every door you knock on as a prospective job interview. The
secret is to knock, knock and knock again.

Another possible source of casual employment in the catering
industry is in the fast-food outlets that have sprouted in almost
every city in the world. Due to the nature of the work staff get
fed-up with great regularity and there are often openings of some
description. Fluency in a foreign language is not always necessary:

if you can master 'cheeseburger', 'french fries' and 'large coke' in a different language then you may be perfectly qualified.

Take a look, too, at other titles in the *How To* series. These are some which can help you:

How to Get a Job Abroad (4th edition), Roger Jones.
How to Teach Abroad (2nd edition), Roger Jones.
How to Get a Job in America (3rd edition), Roger Jones.
How to Get a Job in Australia (2nd edition), Nick Vandome.
How to Get a Job in Europe (3rd edition), Mark Hempshell.
How to Get a Job in Germany, Christine Hall.

Brochures of these and other titles in the series can be obtained from How To Books Ltd, Plymbridge House, Estover Road, Plymouth PL6 7PZ. Tel: (01752) 202301. Fax: (01752) 202331.

Points to consider
- Do you want a job in tourism for an extended period or as a means of making short-term money?
- Do you have any qualifications that would be useful?
- Are you prepared to work long, unsociable hours and do all the dirty jobs going?
- Do you know a foreign language—or are you prepared to learn one?
- Are you prepared to put up with numerous rejections if necessary?
- Be prepared to use your wits—large festivals and sporting events provide excellent opportunities for short-term employment in tourism.

Fruit picking
Although mechanisation is becoming increasingly common in the world of agriculture there are still fruit growers around the globe who are looking for pickers. Whether it is grapes, oranges, apples or tomatoes there are numerous chances for casual employment in this agricultural area. The drawbacks of the job are clear:

- back-breaking work
- long hours
- low pay in most cases
- basic living conditions

For this reason locals in fruit picking areas, from the cherry orchards of the Okanagon in western Canada to the vineyards of the Barossa Valley in Australia, are somewhat reluctant to throw themselves whole-heartedly into the task of picking these produces. Recently, grape farmers in Victoria in Australia had to advertise for pickers in Brisbane, several hundred miles away.

The best areas for prospective fruit pickers are southern Europe, Australia, New Zealand, South Africa and North America. Since many fruit growers are not over-concerned with employment regulations, persistence is sometimes more productive than having the right papers. Local employment agencies (such as the Commonwealth Employment Service in Australia) can direct you to the fruit growing areas of a country and tell you the current employment requirements. If you go to these areas you may be approached in the street and asked if you want a picking job.

Try these exercises to discover the most productive fruit growing areas in the world:

- Check the labels of wine bottles to see which regions of a country they come from.

- Look at the labels of origin of fruits in your local supermarket.

- Check packets of raisins and other dried fruit and see where they come from—dried fruit was once ripe fruit waiting to be picked.

Labouring
If you like fresh air, hard work and working in a team then labouring could be an avenue for casual work. If you have a qualification in a trade, such as a carpenter or an electrician, then you could be in great demand in various parts of the world— there is usually work in Australia for qualified tradesmen. Make sure you take any relevant certificates and references with you.

Even if you do not have a qualification it could be possible to pick up work as a labourer. Wherever there is any sort of construction, be it a new motorway or a holiday resort, there will be various vacancies for casual labourers. These are sometimes on a day-to-day basis and so they are not advertised in newspapers. You can either turn up at the site and ask the foreman if there is any work, or in some cases employment centres recruit casual labourers on a daily basis. The most important thing to note here is that you have to turn up *early*: recruitment is done by taking the first ten or 20 people who have arrived that morning, so being ready by 6am is not an unrealistic target.

It is possible for women to find labouring jobs but you will have to be prepared for the usual discrimination and chauvinism—give as good as you get and you will probably be accepted more readily.

If you are trying to find labouring work points to remember are:

- Find the areas with the most intensive construction.

- Look up building contractors in the *Yellow Pages* and contact them personally.

- Turn up at sites first thing in the morning to see if there is any work.

- Be enthusiastic and willing to do a variety of strenuous and back-breaking jobs.

Factory work
One of the most boring forms of work you are likely to come across, but for that reason it tends to be well paid. There are numerous opportunities throughout Europe, Australia and America, ranging from packing tulips in Holland to processing bananas in Brisbane. A good way to find this type of work is from local newspapers, or else approach the factories directly. The best qualifications are the ability to start early in the morning (or work the night shift) and be able to sit through hours of tedium.

One area which is good for factory work is the fish processing factories in Iceland. Officially you need a work permit but most employers are fairly lenient in this respect. It can be a spartan lifestyle and the work is mind-bogglingly dull—but it is an excellent way to save large sums of money.

Miscellaneous
There are as many types of miscellaneous casual work as there are addresses in a traveller's notebook. Some of the possibilities are:

- Baby sitting—proof of responsibility is useful for this.
- Deck-hand on a prawn trawler.

- Door-to-door salesperson—companies are always looking for thick-skinned individuals to sell anything from encyclopaedias to double-glazing.
- Film extra—particularly in Asia where countries such as India have a massive film industry.
- Jackaroo/Jillaroo on an Australian sheep station.
- Selling time-shares in Spain.

The most important qualities when looking for casual work abroad are:

- flexibility
- initiative
- opportunism
- persistence
- sense of humour

SELLING YOURSELF

When it comes to casual employment it is not necessarily true that everything comes to he who waits. In reality it does not even always come to he who searches the newspapers and goes knocking on doors. Sometimes you have to take the initiative and sell yourself and your employment skills. This can be done in a variety of ways:

1. Placing advertisements in local newspapers. State what you are looking for and what you have to offer. For example: 'Experienced dishwasher seeks dirt and grease to clean in any city hotel or restaurant', or 'Do your lawns need mowing? Your leaves need raking? Or your hedges need trimming? All odd jobs around the garden undertaken. Previously employed by Kew Gardens, London'.

2. Placing similar advertisements in shop windows.

3. Handing out leaflets extolling your virtues as a labourer/ baby-sitter/barman/watch repairer/airline pilot.

4. Promoting yourself verbally. This should not be done in an overbearing fashion: if you hear of an opening then subtly suggest that you could be the person to fill it.

THE COUNTRIES

Some regions of the world are better than others for finding employment in. In some cases it is best to give the idea of working a miss altogether. For an in-depth look at work opportunities around the world, consult the highly informative *How To Get a Job Abroad* (How To Books), or my own *How To Find Temporary Work Abroad* (How To Books).

European Economic Area (EEA)

Austria, Belgium, Denmark, France, Finland, Germany, Greece, Ireland, Italy, Luxembourg, the Netherlands, Norway, Portugal, Spain, Sweden and the UK.

The changes in the employment laws in EEA countries in recent years have made it considerably easier for people from the UK looking for work abroad. The majority of EEA countries have a wide range of openings in tourism, fruit picking, labouring and factory work. You can stay in any EEA country for up to three months looking for work. A good place to start are the national employment services which are similar to our Jobcentres (in France it is the *Agence National pour l'Emploi*, in Germany the *Bundesanstadt für Arbeit*). There are also numerous temporary employment agencies in EEA countries which are worth a try—addresses can be found in local telephone books.

There is a system called The European System for the International Clearing of Vacancies and Applications for Employment (SEDOC) which is designed to help people find jobs in EEA countries. Jobcentres in the UK will be able to provide more information.

Europe—Non-EEA countries

Although there are numerous employment opportunities in these countries you may need a work permit in advance. This does not necessarily cover casual work that you find as you go. If you can find a job that allows you to work unofficially this could be easier than wading through a lot of red tape.

Eastern Europe

With the dramatically changing events in eastern Europe it is still hard to gauge what effect this will have on the employment prospects for travellers. Since in the past these were virtually nil they will inevitably change for the better. At present the best idea would be to monitor closely the situation in eastern Europe and try and get information from the relevant embassies.

European employment requirements
For specific employment requirements in European countries contact:

Albanian Embassy: 6 Wilton Court, 59 Eccleston Square, London SW1X 8PA. Tel: (0171) 235 5252.

Austrian Embassy: 18 Belgrave Mews West, London SW1X 5HU. Tel: (0171) 235 3731.

Embassy of Belarus: 6 Kensington Court, London W8. Tel: (0171) 938 3223.

Belgian Embassy: 103 Eaton Square, London SW1W 9AB. Tel: (0171) 470 3700.

Bosnia-Herzegovina Embassy: 40–41 Conduit Street, London W1R 9FB. Tel: (0171) 743 3758.

Bulgarian Embassy: 186 Queen's Gate, London SW7 5HL. Tel: (0171) 584 9400.

Embassy of Croatia: 21 Conway Street, London W1P. Tel: (0171) 387 1144.

Cyprus High Commission: 93 Park Street, London W1Y 4ET. Tel: (0171) 499 8272.

Czech Embassy: 26 Kensington Palace Gardens, London W8 4QY. Tel: (0171) 243 1115.

Royal Danish Embassy: 55 Sloane Street, London SW1X 9SR. Tel: (0171) 333 0200.

Estonian Embassy: 16 Hyde Park Gate, London SW7 5DG. Tel: (0171) 589 3428.

Finnish Embassy: 38 Chesham Place, London SW1X 8HW. Tel: (0171) 838 6200.

French Embassy: 23 Cromwell Road, London SW7. Tel: (0171) 838 2055.

German Embassy: 23 Belgrave Square, London SW1X 8PZ. Tel: (0171) 824 1300.

Greek Embassy: 1A Holland Park, London W11 3TP. Tel: (0171) 221 6467.

Hungarian Embassy: 35 Eaton Place, London SW1X 8BY. Tel: (0171) 235 4048.

Irish Embassy: 17 Grosvenor Place, London SW1X. Tel: (0171) 235 9371.

Italian Embassy: 14 Three Kings Yard, London W1Y 2EH. Tel: (0171) 312 2200.

Embassy of Latvia: 45 Nottingham Place, London W1M. Tel: (0171) 312 0040.

Lithuanian Embassy: 84 Gloucester Place, London W1H. Tel: (0171) 486 6401.

Macedonian Embassy: 6th Floor, Kingsway House, 103 Kingsway, London WC2B. Tel: (0171) 404 6556.

Malta High Commission: Malta House, 36–38 Piccadily, London W1V. Tel: (0171) 292 4800.

Royal Netherlands Embassy: 38 Hyde Park Gate, London SW7 5DP. Tel: (0171) 584 5040.

Royal Norwegian Embassy: 25 Belgrave Square, London SW1X 8QD. Tel: (0171) 235 7151.

Polish Embassy: 47 Portland Place, London W1N 3AG. Tel: (0171) 580 4324.

Portuguese Embassy: 11 Belgrave Square, London SW1X 8PP. Tel: (0171) 235 5531.

Romanian Embassy: 4 Palace Green, London W8 4QD. Tel: (0171) 937 9666.

Consulate of the Russian Federation: 5 Kensington Palace Gardens, London W8. Tel: (0171) 229 8027.

Embassy of Slovac Republic: 25 Kensington Palace Gardens, London W8. Tel: (0171) 243 0803.

Embassy of Slovenia: Suite 1, Cavendish Court, 11–15 Wigmore Street, London W1H. Tel: (0171) 495 7775.

Spanish Embassy: 39 Chesham Place, London SW1X. Tel: (0171) 235 5555.

Swedish Embassy: 11 Montagu Place, London W1H 2AL. Tel: (0171) 917 6400.

Swiss Embassy: 16–18 Montagu Place, London W1H 2AL. Tel: (0171) 616 6000.

Turkish Embassy: 43 Belgrave Square, London SW1X 8AP. Tel: (0171) 393 0202.

Embassy of Ukraine: 78 Kensington Park Road, London W11. Tel: (0171) 727 6312.

Yugoslav Embassy: 5/7 Lexham Gardens, London W8 5JJ. Tel: (0171) 370 6105.

Australia

One of the best locations for work during a year abroad. Although the Australian economy has been suffering over recent years there are still vacancies in areas such as tourism, fruit picking and labouring. Despite their 'whinging Pom' tag the Brits are usually considered good workers and you should never be short of work for too long here.

The best way to qualify for employment in Australia is to apply for a **Working Holiday Visa**. This is valid for a maximum of a year and you are eligible if:

1. You are aged between 18 and 25.
2. You want to travel in Australia and supplement your income with periods of employment for a maximum of three months in one place.
3. You hold a valid UK, Irish, Canadian or Dutch passport.
4. You have enough money for a return ticket and to support yourself for the first few months of your stay. (This is approximately £2000 for a year) and you will have to produce an original bank statement and not merely a statement showing the account total. Any large sums paid into your account must be explained.

There is a charge of £78 for a Working Holiday Visa and you should not apply more than four weeks prior to your proposed departure date. You can only have a Working Holiday Visa once so make sure that you are going to take full advantage of it.

Once you are in Australia you may want to use the **Commonwealth Employment Service** (CES) in your job search. This is the Australian equivalent of the Jobcentre. Newspapers such as the *Melbourne Age*, the *Sydney Herald* and the Brisbane *Courier and Mail* have extensive sections of classified advertisements for casual employment. For additional information and contacts, consult Laura Veltman's *How to Live & Work in Australia* (5th edition 1996) and my own book *How to Get a Job in Australia* (2nd edition 1995)—both published in this series.

Suggested jobs and regions
- Apple picking—Tasmania, Western Australia
- Banana picking—Queensland
- Grape picking—New South Wales, Victoria, South Australia, Western Australia.
- Jackaroo—any outback sheep station

- Mining—Western Australia, South Australia
- Prawn fishing—Northern Territory and northern Queensland
- Tourism—Queensland (northern Queensland and the Gold Coast near Brisbane), Northern Territory (Ayers Rock and Alice Springs).

Australian visas can be obtained from:

Australian High Commission
   Australia House
   The Strand
   London WC2B 4LA
or

Australian Consulate
   Chatsworth House
   Lever Street
   Manchester M1 2QL
or

Australian Embassy
   Fitzwilton House
   Wilton Terrace
   Dublin
   Ireland

New Zealand

Work permits are harder to obtain than in Australia but it is possible to get one for casual work if you write to the nearest Immigration Service when in the country. However, this can be costly and tiresome. An easier way is to obtain a tax number (this can be done by going to the nearest Inland Revenue Department and asking for one) and showing this to potential employers.

As a rule it should be possible to find casual work in New Zealand, but do not abuse the system. For further information:

New Zealand Immigration Service
   3rd Floor
   New Zealand House
   80 Haymarket
   London SW1Y 4TE

United States of America

It is notoriously difficult to find casual work in America legally. If you want to be official the best idea is BUNAC's Work America scheme (see Chapter 2).

Other than this, unless you can arrange an **H1-B Temporary Worker Visa** (which has to be done through an American employer before you enter the country and can take up to eight months), a B-1 Voluntary Work Visa or a Q Visa (an International Cultural Exchange Visa which is valid for up to 15 months) you can only work illegally. Due to the range of job opportunities —from barman in Disney World to ski instructor in Colorado—a lot of people do this. However, there are a few points to consider:

1. Make sure you have adequate funds when you enter the country: at least $500 for every month of your proposed stay plus credit cards. Immigration officers are always on the look-out for impoverished travellers who are hoping to finance their time in America through casual work.

2. Due to new laws social security cards now need to be physically inspected by employers so you cannot just think up a number. Some people may be willing to take your word for it though.

3. Be on the look-out for immigration officials, particularly if you are in an area where there are large numbers of illegal workers— such as Florida and Texas.

4. If employers are unscrupulous enough to take on illegal labour they may be unscrupulous in other ways too.

Canada

The story here is similar to America although there has been a certain amount of relaxation in recent years with regard to casual summer employment. These are official work exchange schemes and applicants must be British citizens aged 18 to 30 and be returning to tertiary education in Britain. For more information contact:

Canadian High Commission
  1 Grosvenor Square
  London W1X 0AB

Two *How To* books can also help you, Roger Jones's *How to Get a Job in America* (3rd ed. 1995) and *Applying for an American Visa*, by the American immigration lawyer Richard Fleischer.

Africa, Asia and Latin America

For a number of reasons, such as large local work forces, local regulations and unstable economies, the chance of getting casual work in these countries is little better than zero. You may find a few days work as a film extra or a model but you should not rely on employment if you are travelling in these areas. In many ways you don't need to because the cost of living and travelling is invariably so cheap that you would not achieve any great financial gain by working.

If you do want to work in Third World countries then your best bets are:

● Teaching English as a Foreign Language.
● Working for a voluntary organisation.

GO FOR THE UNUSUAL

Whatever type of casual work you do, try at least once to do something that you would not have the chance to do at home. Working in a bar in Sydney may be enjoyable and financially rewarding but will it be so different from working in a bar in London or Glasgow? Instead of spending three months as a waiter do it for six weeks and then spend the rest of the time on a prawn trawler or scrabbling about picking grapes. Seeing a different side of life is one of the great joys of a year abroad.

CHECKLIST

1. Do you need a work permit for the countries in which you are intending to look for casual work?
2. Do you know the consequences of working illegally in various countries?
3. Do you know where to locate the official centres for finding casual work?
4. Have you gained any relevant experience at home?
5. If not, can you convince employers that you would be an asset to their business?
6. Will you be treating casual work as a financial necessity or as

a means to earn some extra cash while you put down roots for a while?

7. Do you want to do something that is out of the ordinary?
8. Are you prepared to keep looking for work if you do not succeed immediately?
9. Will you take the initiative in the job search?
10. Are you prepared to turn your hand to anything?

How to Get a Job Abroad
Roger Jones BA(Hons) DipEd DPA

Fourth Edition

This great value-for-money paperback guide is essential reading for everyone planning to spend a period abroad. A key feature is the lengthy reference section of medium and long-term job opportunities and possibilities, arranged by region and country of the world, and by profession/occupation. There are many more than 130 pages of specific contacts and leads, giving literally hundreds of addresses and much hard-to-find information. There is a classified guide to overseas recruitment agencies, and even a multi-lingual guide to writing application letters. The first edition of this popular handbook was published in 1989, and has since sold many thousands of copies. The book has now been thoroughly revised and updated into a fourth edition: it contains many new addresses and entries, and reflects recent political developments in Europe, the Gulf, and other parts of the world.

From Reviews

'A fine book for anyone considering even a temporary overseas job.' *The Evening Star*. 'A highly informative and well researched book . . . containing lots of hard information and a first class reference section . . . A superb buy.' *The Escape Committee Newsletter*. Roger Jones BA AKC DipTESL DipEd MInstAm DPA MBIM has himself worked abroad for many years in such varied locations as Austria, Cambodia, Thailand, Turkey and the Middle East. A specialist writer on expatriate and employment matters, he is also author of **How to Teach Abroad** in the same series.

£9.99pb, 272pp illus. 1 85703 182 2. 4th edition

How To Books Ltd, Plymbridge House, Estover Road, Plymouth PL6 7PZ, United Kingdom. Tel: (01752) 202301. Fax: (01752) 202331. Telex: 45635.

5
Trying Freelance Work

WRITING AS YOU GO

It is a romantic notion to dream of making money from writing as you travel around the world. The good news is that this is a definite possibility, but the downside is that there are a lot of people competing for the privilege.

Questions to answer before you go
- Are you going to be writing fiction or non-fiction?
- Will you be sending articles back to Britain or trying to sell them in the countries you visit?
- Will you be writing as you go or just taking notes for later?
- Have you written anything before?

Non-fiction is king
The majority of articles in magazines, and particularly newspapers, are non-fiction. We have, it seems, an insatiable appetite for factual information and if you are thinking seriously about making money from your time abroad this will be your best option.

Within the field of non-fiction there is a vast array of topics to write about. The most obvious of these is, of course, travel. A word of warning about this though—everyone you see abroad with a pen in their hand will be writing travel articles. It is an *extremely* competitive market and even if you are good at it most newspapers and magazines are oversubscribed with submissions. Despite this it is worth doing some travel writing, even if it is ultimately for your own enjoyment. There are a number of points to consider with this type of work:

- Write in the first person—people will want to read about what you think and feel father than guidebook platitudes.

- Avoid purple prose and clichés. Sometimes the simple sentence is the best one.

- Do not be afraid to use humour—travelling is supposed to be fun after all.

- Use anecdotes and direct speech to break up your prose.

- Try and convey the feel of a country or an area.

- Find your own voice. If you try and copy someone else's style then you will only sound derivative and stilted.

- Always send a query letter before submitting the actual article. Give an outline of the proposed article and state any previous writing credits. This will save you a considerable amount of time if the publication in question already has material covering this topic.

Who might be interested in my work?
Some outlets to consider for travel articles:

The *Daily Telegraph*
   Peterborough Court
   South Quay Plaza
   181 Marsh Wall
   London E14 9SR
   Tel: (0171) 538 5000
Travel editor: Gill Charlton.

The *Guardian*
   119 Farringdon Road
   London EC1R 3ER
   Tel: (0171) 278 2332
Travel editor: Jeannette Page.

The *Independent*
   1 Canada Square
   Canary Wharf
   London E14 5DL
   Tel: (0171) 345 2000
Travel editor: Simon Calder.

The *Scotsman*
  20 North Bridge
  Edinburgh EH1 1YT
  Tel: (0131) 225 2468
  Travel editor: Alistair McKay.

Traveller
  WEXAS International
  45–49 Brompton Road
  Knightsbridge
  London SW3 1DE
  Tel: (0171) 589 3315
Travel Editor: Miranda Haines.

Trailfinder
  42–50 Earls Court Road
  London W8 6EJ
  Tel: (0171) 937 8499
Managing editor: Heidi Gardner.

The Lady
  39–40 Bedford Street
  The Strand
  London WC2E 9ER
  Tel: (0171) 379 4717
Editor: Arline Usden.

What should I write about?
Before submitting any article read the targeted publication very carefully. Study the articles they publish for style, length and tone. Do not be too discouraged if your work is rejected—as well as the great number of submissions they receive, many newspapers and magazines are trying to cut costs by generating their travel material in-house.

Although it is perfectly possible that you will succeed in selling travel articles it is a good idea to consider other areas of non-fiction:

● Conservation—logging in Indonesia or Australia perhaps.
● Education—there are hundreds of unique and unusual schools around the world.
● Food and drink—a topic close to most people's hearts.

- Sport—as sumo and American football gain in popularity in Britain there must be other sports around the world that could be brought to our attention.
- Politics.
- Economics.
- Social issues—prostitution in Thailand or homelessness in America.

Britain or abroad

There is no reason why you cannot sell articles in both Britain and the countries in which you are travelling (as long as it is relevant to both).

For British markets consult the two 'bibles' for writers:

- *The Writers' and Artists' Year Book* (A & C Black)
- *The Writer's Handbook* (Macmillan/PEN)

These not only include all the major British newspapers and magazines but also some publications in Europe and the Commonwealth. For all-important tips on how to market your work successfully, see Chriss McCallum's book *How to Write for Publication* (How To Books, 3rd edition 1995).

Down Under and the US

If you are interested in writing for American or Australian markets (the two most lucrative areas abroad) then it would be a good idea to get hold of:

- *The Writer's Market US*, Writers' Digest Books, F & W Publications, 1057 Dana Avenue, Cincinnati, Ohio 45207.

- *The Writers' and Photographers' Market Guide for Australia and New Zealand*, Australian Writers' Professional Services, PO Box 28, Collins Street, Melbourne, Victoria 3001.

Not only do these two books list the most useful markets for freelancers but they also include some basic facts that a writer likes to know, such as editorial requirements and rates of pay.

The Australian markets are some of the most promising, for two reasons:

1. Except for the odd 'struth' and 'fair dinkum', they talk, and write, in a similar fashion to ourselves. This means that you do not have to worry about unusual spellings or grammar—you can write in exactly the same way as you would for a UK publication.
2. Per capita, Australia probably has a wider range of magazines than anywhere else in the world. There seems to be an equivalent for every British publication, and with a quarter of the population this makes good odds for freelancers from overseas.

The American side of things is not quite so promising. True, there are thousands of potential markets (over 4000 in the *Writer's Market*) but the style of many of them is a bit different to the UK. They go for a much bolder, 'grab you by the throat', approach and this should be kept in mind not only when submitting articles but also with query letters. There is no room for pussy-footing around, so say what you mean and say it as punchily and as positively as possible.

Africa and Asia
African and Asian markets are unlikely to make you rich quick— some may not even pay you at all—but if you are planning a visit to any of these countries it would be worth getting in touch with the editors of the English language newspapers in these places. If nothing else it may give you a contact in a strange country.

Europe
The humble travelling writer has benefited from the introduction of the single European market. With Europe being viewed as a single trade entity there will be every opportunity to make sales throughout the European Union. This can be done either through syndicates or the personal approach. Syndicates covering Europe can be found in the *Writers' and Artists' Yearbook* and they will generally take anything they think will attract a European editor. Boom subjects on the continent these days are business, information technology, science and medicine—so basically, if you can write about money-generating subjects then you stand a good chance of generating some yourself.

If you want to approach European magazines on your own then the system is the same as for any other overseas markets. Consult

Willings Press Guide (British Media Publications) for a list of European publications.

Writing on the road

Travelling is a time-consuming and sometimes stressful occupation at the best of times. If you are trying to incorporate writing at the same time this can be an added burden. You will have two main considerations to face:

1. How and where to write.
2. How to get it to publications in a suitable form.

Due to necessity you will probably have to write your articles with pen and paper. For many this may not be a problem, but for the committed typewriter- or PCW-user it could be a novel experience. Due to the nature of travelling it is a good idea to utilise the many hours you will have to kill while waiting for transport; many articles have been drafted in airports or bus stations.

Whether you write completed articles while you are travelling or make notes to be written up later is entirely up to the individual. Some people like the immediacy of writing while things are fresh in their mind, while others prefer to leave things until they can put them in a proper perspective. Whatever you do make sure that you take detailed notes—the human memory has an unfortunate habit of forgetting the most important facts at the most vital moments.

The question of presentation is a vexed one for the travelling writer. Material *must* be typed on one side of the paper and double-spaced. This gives you three options:

1. Hope you make some contacts who can point you in the direction of a typewriter or a computer. If you do get this chance then grab it with both hands.
2. Send your material home to a reliable friend or relation, asking them if they could type it up for you and send it to the relevant publication.
3. Wait until you get back home to submit your material.

How can I get experience?

Several writing careers have been conceived as a result of time spent abroad, so experience beforehand is not essential. Having said this it would be advantageous to have some experience. If you have not done any serious writing then you can:

- Enrol in a nightclass.
- Consult the magazines *Writers' Monthly*, 29 Turnpike Lane, London N8 0EP. Tel: (0181) 342 8879 and *Writers News*, PO Box 4, Nairn IV12 4HU. Tel: (01667) 454441.
- Read as much as possible of the type of writing you are hoping to emulate.
- Write, write and write again.

Other writing options

Writing a non-fiction book
If you can write a non-fiction article see if you have enough material to expand it into a full-length book. As with articles the most obvious form is a travel book and, if you have the talent, it can be an easier task to sway publishers than newspaper editors.

Writing a fiction book
Fiction need not be excluded from the writing-and-travelling scenario. With the numerous locations you visit and the people you meet you will be able to gather ideas for all manner of books, from novels to detective stories.

Writing guidebooks
Logically enough, most guidebooks are written by travellers. If you are interested in this type of work then write to the publishers offering your services. You will need to send a detailed synopsis of what you are offering and where you are going to be travelling. Even if you are not commissioned to write an entire book you may be asked to submit material on a certain area or a specific town.

Checklist of writing material
1. Pen and notebook that are easily accessible at *all* times.
2. Names and addresses of editors and publications in the countries you will be visiting.
3. Names and addresses of editors and publications in Britain.
4. A dictaphone—for jotting down your ideas and also for con-

ducting any interviews. Be careful with these going through customs since the more paranoid officers may think you are a spy.

5. A rabbit's foot for luck—the one piece of essential equipment for a writer.

Summary

Don't — limit your writing to travel writing
— submit handwritten material
— write articles at inappropriate times
— copy someone else's style
— be too down-hearted by rejection.

Do — find your own voice
— pick topics in which you have a particular interest
— take notes as often as possible
— use your spare time for writing and rewriting
— try, try and try again.

USING PHOTOGRAPHY

Most travellers take cameras with them and for the enthusiast it makes sense to try and turn a hobby into hard cash. If you are successful you may even find a new career for yourself.

Will I need an expensive camera?

Not necessarily. Having an auto-focus, auto-wind, auto-teamaking camera does not ensure that you will take good photographs. It is a subject that is very much in the eye of the beholder and you can take photographs of a publishable quality with a standard 35mm single lens reflex (SLR) camera and a couple of lenses. Also, the more auto features that a camera has the more there is to go wrong. It may be difficult to get spare parts if you are in the middle of the Amazonian jungle.

Another point to consider is that if you are walking about with a £500 camera hanging around your neck you are making yourself a hostage to fortune. It will be worth more than some of the people you meet earn in a year. For some, the temptation to part you from your camera, by whatever means, may be too great to resist.

Equipment to take
Unless you want to specialise in one aspect of photography, such as wildlife or botany, the basic equipment you will need is:

- 35mm SLR camera body. These vary in price but a good quality one such as Canon, Pentax or Minolta can be bought second-hand for anything from £100 upwards;
- a wide-angle lens. This is the standard lens and should be between 28mm and 50mm;
- a zoom lens, 70-210mm;
- a 2x convertor. This is an accessory which doubles the focal length of a lens, so your zoom lens would become 140-420mm. There is a slight loss of definition with this so it is worthwhile buying one of reasonable quality;
- camera bag—some travellers like a bag that does not look like a camera bag, to deter inquisitive eyes, but the standard ones are undoubtedly better for the job;
- polarising filter;
- ultra-violet filter;
- silica gel—to protect the equipment from humidity;
- flash gun;
- tripod—optional.

This is just the basics of equipment. It is vital to do a certain amount of photography before you go and experiment with various lenses to see which suits you the best.

Film
The best type of film for reproduction in magazines is colour transparency (slides) while newspapers traditionally prefer black and white prints. However, as photographic publishing technology marches towards the 21st century and beyond it is becoming increasingly common to find good quality colour print film being accepted. As a rule it is a good idea to get in touch with relevant publications first and ask their requirements for photographic material.

For general use Kodachrome 64 is the most commonly used film for transparencies while Ilford do a range of good quality black and white print film. If you are taking pictures in poor light you could try Kodachrome 200 Professional.

Before you go

If you are serious about making money from photography it is a
good idea to do some groundwork before you go. Decide what type
of photographs you want to take and then look at magazines and
newspapers to see who publishes this type of material. When it
comes to selling your work you could either try the direct approach
or you could deal with an agent (see below).

Subjects to shoot

You will be faced with a myriad of visual images while you are
travelling and the hardest thing may be to avoid shooting off dozens
of films in the first few days. Although you should have a rough
idea of the areas you want to specialise in you should always be
aware of the one shot that may keep you in caviar and champagne
for the rest of your life. Opportunism is one of the most important
pieces of equipment a photographer can carry: the lucky snapper
who caught the moment when Pope John Paul II was shot is
probably still living off the proceeds of that one picture. If you
manage to get such a picture (including moments of natural
disaster) you should take it to the office of the nearest news agency
(for instance Reuters or United Press International) and begin
serious negotiations.

Other subjects to consider are:

Landscapes

Try to avoid large expanses of greens and blues. Look for features
that will brighten a landscape photograph and act as a focus of
attention. Be careful of sunsets—they always look wonderful at the
time but can become slightly monotonous after you have looked at
several dozen of them on film.

People

There is a large market for portrait photographs of people around
the world. Remember to ask permission before you take this type
of picture.

Wildlife

Particularly worthwhile in Africa. For this type of work you may
need additional equipment such as a tele-photo lens.

Architecture
This can include various types of buildings since photograph libraries use all manner of pictures.

Sport
A competitive field but worth considering, particularly if you come across unusual or unknown sports.

Storms
Not all good photographs are taken in brilliant sunlight. There is a large market for dramatic photographs taken in bad weather.

If you decide to specialise in one area, for instance the sea and its surroundings, you may have a better chance of carving a niche for yourself in the world of photography.

What not to photograph
Unfortunately, more than one photographer has had to endure a spell in a foreign prison as a result of pointing his camera in the wrong direction. Many countries have strict rules about what you can and cannot photograph. Find these out for each of your destinations before you go. In some cases you may have to obtain a photographic permit. Some of the areas that you will have to be careful of are:

- military installations
- troop movements
- oil refineries
- airfields
- civil engineering works
- scenes that show a country to be primitive
- bridges—strategic points during times of war.

If you are arrested for snapping something that is off-limits you may get away with paying a bribe and having your film confiscated. If it appears to be a serious offence you should try to get in contact with the nearest British Embassy as quickly as possible.

Respect the locals
Some cultures and races believe that if you take their photograph then you steal their spirit. Whether you believe this or not you

should respect their wishes and not photograph them. Do not try to take a surreptitious photograph either—this is insulting to all concerned and could lead to a nasty confrontation. One American traveller recently tried to take a secret photograph of a tribesman in northern Kenya—and got a spear through the chest for his troubles.

One side-effect of world tourism is that many local people have compromised their principles and offer their services to photographers—at a price. Again, it is not for us to judge them and if this is their wish then photographers should meet their demands. In some cases, such as the Masai in Kenya, the price of a photograph can be as much as £20. It is up to the photographer to decide whether this is worth it in terms of what they may realise for the picture.

Selling your photographs

In most instances it will be best to wait until you return home to try to sell your work. You can do this in two ways:

1. Through a photographic agency or library.
2. On your own.

Agencies
These have a number of advantages:
- They deal regularly with picture editors, picture researchers and art buyers.
- They know the needs and changes in the market trends.
- They know the different markets such as calendars, postcards and travel brochures—travel photography is not just for newspapers and magazines.
- They can deal with the minefield of photographic copyright.
- They can get the best price for your work—novices in this field often sell their work for less than it is worth.

If you want to investigate the possibility of being taken on by a picture library or an agency you should consult the *The Freelance Photographers Market Handbook* to see which agencies deal with different types of photographs. You should then send a covering letter, asking if they are interested in taking on more photographers and detailing what type of work you are offering. If they are interested you will be asked to send an initial sample of at least

200 photographs. (This is one case when colour pictures *must* be submitted as transparencies, and preferably in a larger format than the standard 35mm.) You should also indicate how many photographs you think you will be able to supply over a period of time. If you are taken on you can expect to get up to £100 for a single photograph (and in some cases considerably more) and agents can sell the same image several times over.

Presentation of work is important when you are applying to agencies. A few basic rules should be followed:

● Never send work you consider to be anything less than your best—it will be rejected swiftly and only detract from the rest of your work.

● Always include detailed captions. These should be typed on a separate sheet of paper and include: the photographer's name and address, the country and area where the photograph was taken and a brief description of the subject. For instance—'Australia: Northern Territory. Camel races in Alice Springs'. With transparencies this should also be written on the frame in indelible ink.

● Transparencies should be sent in plastic wallets and prints should be sent in card-stiffened envelopes.

If your work is taken on by an agency you should insure it against loss or damage.

Agencies and photograph libraries which specialise in travel photography include:

PictureBank Photo Library
  Parman House
  30–36 Fife Road
  Kingston upon Thames
  Surrey KT1 1SY
  Tel: (0181) 547 2344

Impact Photos
  26–7 Great Sutton Street
  London EC1V 0DX
  Tel: (0171) 251 5091

Raleigh International
Picture Library
  Raleigh House
  27 Parsons Green Lane
  London SW6 4HS
  Tel: (0171) 371 8585

Pictures Colour Library
  10A Neale's Yard
  London WC2H 9DP
  Tel: (0171) 497 2034

Reuter and UPI
  c/o Popperphoto
  The Old Mill
  Overstone Farm
  Overstone
  Northampton NN6 0AB
  Tel: (01604) 670670

The Photographer's Library
  81A Endell Street
  London WC2H 9AJ
  Tel: (0171) 836 5591

On your own

If you choose to try to sell your work yourself you could set up your own picture library (you may want to do this if you have a large number of photographs on a specialist subject) or approach magazines and newspapers directly. This has disadvantages compared to going through an agency:

- You will have fewer markets available to you.
- You will be looked upon as a keen amateur rather than a professional.
- You may not be paid as much for your work.

However, if you just want to see some of your photographs in print this could be the best idea. If you submit photographs to illustrate any articles you write make sure that you are paid separately. Some publications, including national newspapers, seem to think that the words and the pictures come in a package together and pay you accordingly.

Summary
- Take good quality equipment but not excessively expensive—second-hand purchases are a good buy.
- Find out if you need a photography permit for where you are going.
- Never take pictures of politically or militarily sensitive subjects.
- If you want to be taken on by an agency you will need a large number of high-quality photographs.
- Always keep a record of the pictures you take.
- Always ask permission to take pictures of local people.

MAKING THE MOST OF OTHER FREELANCE OPPORTUNITIES

Making the most of your talents

Earning money from freelance work often depends on your own initiative and willingness to stick your neck out, as Tammi Dallaston Wood found in Asia:

> 'Identify a need and offer to fill it—whether it be teaching English in exchange for board, or designing a menu for the restaurant you frequent in return for a couple of meals. If you offer your skills and services freely, you can usually be expected to be generously rewarded without asking. If you have a particular skill, especially an artistic one, take the tools of the trade with you.'

Busking

If you can sing, play the guitar, juggle chain-saws or tap dance in green wellies then you could turn to busking to earn some extra money. Make sure you know the local laws regarding this before you start and be prepared to be moved along by the police. Stick to areas where there are large crowds, such as shopping areas or outside large sporting events. Try to make your act original and do not encroach too near to other buskers.

Gambling

Perhaps not the safest way to make some extra cash but worth thinking about if you are an expert poker player or can do a few card tricks such as 'Spot the Lady'. Whenever you win money gambling there is always the risk that the loser will turn nasty, so a quick tongue and an even quicker pair of legs are invaluable when you are engaged in this type of activity.

Selling

If you make jewellery, design T-shirts or paint watercolours you could set up a small stall. Again, there may be local regulations regarding this so you should enquire as to whether you need a permit. Otherwise make sure you keep one step ahead of the authorities.

One potentially lucrative area for selling is food. You can do this yourself by setting up a stall selling cold drinks, sandwiches or chocolate but this might not ingratiate you with the local traders.

Alternatively you could sell items for someone else and take a commission on each sale. This is popular among ice-cream companies in Australia—you are given a tray full of ice-cream, pointed towards the nearest beach and told to sell, sell, sell. Even working on a commission basis you can make a lot of money this way: John Shinner from Surrey did this in Sydney and earned $A100 a day—plus all the ice-cream he could eat.

Street painting
In tourist areas it is increasingly common to see areas of pavement covered in large pastel paintings of anything from the Beatles to Van Gogh's 'Sunflowers'. If you have a knack for drawing, a good set of pastel crayons and an ability to stop people walking on the designated piece of pavement then this could be a lucrative sideline.

CHECKLIST FOR FREELANCE WORK

1. Treat it as a hobby but be aware that it could turn into a full-time career.
2. Aim small and hope to expand.
3. Practise writing/photography/busking before you leave.
4. Always be on the lookout for topics for your freelance work.
5. Be prepared to work 24 hours a day—a freelancer's mind never has a day off.
6. Don't be afraid to dream.
7. Balance your dreams with a healthy dose of reality.
8. Always look for the unusual and the original.
9. Keep up your freelance work when you return home—it may finance another year abroad.
10. Stick to your guns and don't let other people discourage you.

6
Experiencing the Joy of Travel

To some people the process of getting to a destination is merely an inconvenience that has to be endured in order to spend two weeks soaking on a Mediterranean beach. To others, most notably the independent traveller, it is a joy in itself, to be savoured and relished.

A substantial part of any year abroad (in some cases the entire year) is going to be spent travelling in one form or another and so it is best to undertake a certain amount of planning beforehand to ensure that it is as enjoyable an experience as possible.

DOING THE GROUNDWORK

It is important to know a certain amount about any country that you plan to visit and travel in. This is vital as far as official considerations, such as visas, are concerned but it is also important to have a 'feel' for a country before you go there. This is not only common courtesy; if you know a bit about the history, customs, language and way of life of the place you are visiting then you will feel more at ease when you arrive.

Things to ask yourself

Who do I know (or could find) who has been there?
If you want to know the type of food eaten in northern Tibet or the dress codes of Malawi the best idea is to talk to people who have been there. Not only will they be able to give you practical advice about the types of transport, accommodation and official-dom, they will also have words of wisdom and hints that may not necessarily appear in guidebooks. You can learn so much from facts and figures in a book, but it is invaluable to speak to someone who can explain the realities of spending ten hours picking grapes in

Australia, or how border guards in Brazil administer yellow fever injections.

Finding people from your family and friends who have been to the countries you plan to visit may at first seem a distant prospect. However, if you ask around you will inevitably find someone who knows a workmate, a friend, or a schoolteacher who has been to the country in question. Even if they are unknown to you, get in touch with them and ask if you can talk to them about their experiences. Travellers are usually delighted to talk about what they have done and listening to a first-person account is the best way to generate enthusiasm for a trip.

Do I know any resident of the country?
The prospect of coming across a resident of Bolivia or Singapore may seem even more unlikely than the chances of a friend having been there. However, there are people from all over the world in every city in Britain, and the best place to find them is at your local university. Most universities have an Overseas Students department and if you contact them, telling them what you are looking for, they will be able to put you in touch with people from the country in question. This will not only provide you with invaluable information but it could also lead to some useful contacts in the countries you are visiting.

You can also find out about your destination by consulting:

- guidebooks
- travel literature
- newspapers.

Guidebooks
Guidebooks are invaluable to the traveller—if used properly. They can give you a wealth of information covering history, places to see, transport and accommodation. But they should be used as a guide, not as a bible to be followed religiously. Remember, hundreds of other people will be using the same guide as you and, unless you want to become part of the herd on the tourist route, you should use guidebooks discerningly: stay in some hotels and camp grounds that are not mentioned, visit areas that are not dealt with, and find new restaurants and cafes in which to eat. This is the way new places are discovered and you can enjoy your own unique experiences.

Some of the major guidebook series are:

- **Lonely Planet**. Lonely Planet Publications, PO Box 617, Hawthorn, Victoria 3122, Australia. Written by travellers for travellers. They produce two series of guides—*On a Shoestring*, which cover several countries, such as South-East Asia or Africa, and *Travel Survival Kits*, which cover individual countries. Over 100 titles cover most areas of the world, although the coverage of European countries is slightly less extensive. The guides are written in a down-to-earth, honest style and pull no punches. Updated every two to three years and one of the best investments for an independent traveller.
- **Rough Guides**. Rough Guides Ltd, 1 Mercer Street, London WC2H 9QT. Similar to Lonely Planet in style but with 47 titles their range is not yet as far-reaching. Good coverage of Europe and also parts of Africa, the USA and Central and South America. Introductory information covering the countries involved and recommendations for the low-priced choices in travel, accommodation and food. Updated every two years, competitively priced and gaining in popularity with travellers.
- **Cadogan Guides**. Cadogan Books, Letts House, Parkgate Road, London SW11 4NQ. Strong coverage of European destinations. Stylishly written and presented, they are aimed at a wide range of travellers, from the independent to the lavish. Worth looking into at the library to see if it will be useful for your purposes.
- **Bradt Publications**. 41 Nortoft Road, Chalfont St Peter, Bucks SL9 0LA. Tel: (01494) 873 478. A valuable *Backpacking Guides* series and now expanding into more general guidebooks for some of the more unusual destinations such as Madagascar and Vietnam. Written by experienced travellers who have been there, done it, and sometimes done it again.
- **Let's Go Guides**. Harvard Student Agencies Inc, 1 Story Street, Cambridge, Mass 02138, USA. Written by Harvard students and updated annually. Cover Europe and America and designed to show you how to get the most for your money.
- **Vacation Work**. 9 Park End Street, Oxford OX1 1HJ. Tel: (01865) 241 978. Publishers of the invaluable *Work Your Way Around the World* and other useful titles for employment and

study abroad. They are now branching out into *Travel Survival Kits*. Aimed at the budget traveller and written in the same entertaining, practical style as the rest of the Vacation Work titles.

● **Travel and Trade Publications.** 5 Prince's Buildings, George Street, Bath BA21 2ED. Tel: (01225) 469141. Publish numerous continental travel guides, including the *South America Handbook*, the recognised authority on this part of the world.

● **Fodor's Guides.** Aimed at the more affluent tourist looking for a bit of luxury. Worth looking at for their practical information, which is of a high standard, and for ideas when you want to splurge a little. Updated annually and more useful than its critics sometimes suggest.

Pocket guides

The number of publishers producing pocket guidebooks has increased in recent years. The advantages are obvious—size—and they contain a surprising amount of information, particularly if you are planning a short-stay visit. The major series are:

● **American Express pocket guides**—recognised as the best available.
● **Berlitz**
● **Collins Travellers**
● **AA's Essential Guides**
● **Insight Pocket Guides**

By their very nature guidebooks are not 100 per cent accurate and none of them claim to be. The considerable delay between the time of writing and the publication date means that prices will have increased, timetables will have been altered and, in certain cases, the political climate may have changed dramatically— guidebooks covering the Soviet Union may now seem somewhat dated.

All these factors should be taken into account when you are reading a guidebook—do not take everything it says as gospel. If you do come across any errors or omissions then you can help the publishers by writing to them and pointing out the changes. They are always delighted to receive this type of information and you may even get a mention in the next edition.

Travel literature

In the last ten years there has been a huge increase in the volume of travel writing being published; the neutral observer could be forgiven for thinking that it is a prerequisite for travellers to produce a book at the end of their wanderings. Few parts of the world have been excluded from this process and it is now possible to experience the world from the comfort of your own living-room.

However, travel literature is not only enjoyable for the armchair traveller, it is also useful for conveying the spirit of a country to people who are planning a visit. You may not pick up too much practical advice from a travel book but you will hear the sounds, smell the smells and feel the sun on your back. There is nothing like a good travel book to inspire a case of wanderlust.

Whether you read classics of travel literature such as Patrick Leigh Fermor or Wilfred Thesiger, or the modern works of Colin Thubron, Paul Theroux and Jonathan Raban, or the humorous works of Redmond O'Hanlon, it is worth dipping into a certain amount of travel literature before you go. It might even give you some ideas for a book of your own.

Newspapers

All the quality daily and Sunday newspapers carry travel sections, which are usually a mixture of first-person accounts and practical advice. These have the great advantage of being reasonably up-to-date and most of them carry valuable Fact Packs about the regions written about.

News pages should also be consulted, in order to find out if there has just been a coup in the country you intend to visit or if an earthquake has struck a region you plan to travel through.

QUALITY NOT QUANTITY

Should I try to put down roots?

Although a lot can be fitted into a year it is not a competition to see how many countries you can visit in 12 months. If you treat it as a whistle-stop tour of the world then you will see a great deal, but learn very little.

As the respected traveller and writer Dervla Murphy says in *The Traveller's Handbook*:

'Many [youngsters] seem to cover too much ground too quickly, sampling everywhere but becoming familiar with nowhere. It would be good if this fashion soon changed, if the young became more discriminating, allowing themselves time to travel seriously in a small area that they had chosen because of its particular appeal to them.'

This is good advice for anyone—better to get to know one area and the people very well, rather than move transiently through a large number of different countries and cultures. There is nothing better than being accepted into a community in a different country, but this takes time for both parties to come to terms with the idea. Conversely, it can be very dispiriting to constantly feel as if you are looking at a country through a pane of thick glass, unable to break down the barrier because of a desire to keep moving.

Travelling is as much about knowing when to stop as it is about motion. You will be doing yourself, and those around you, a favour if you resist the desire to try and obtain as many stamps in your passport as possible. Mass tourism, with its emphasis on quantity, has done much to spoil several parts of the world; the independent traveller can redress the balance slightly by showing that they can be sympathetic and understanding to the ways and wishes of others.

SHOULD I GO IT ALONE?

London's Earl Court is famous for being a mini-Australia. Antipodean travellers gravitate towards this Aussie suburb, where they mix with their fellow countrymen, drink Fosters in Australian pubs and even have their own magazines. Is this really what you want after you have travelled 10,000 miles?

While there will be times when you are grateful for the company of travellers from home, it is usually advisable to avoid your fellow countrymen as much as possible. This is sometimes easier said than done, but you will gain significant benefits if you can associate with locals as much as possible: you will be accepted a lot quicker, you will get to know a place in more detail and you will experience more of a sense of 'belonging'.

It is also advisable to avoid the 'pack instinct' that sometimes prevails among travellers. It can be very intimidating for locals to be faced with a large number of strangers. They are much more likely to be welcoming if they have to contend with smaller numbers.

Making local contacts

Contacts in a country you are visiting can make all the difference.
You can either make them beforehand through friends or relations
or you can make valuable contacts once you are in a country.

If you are given names and addresses before you go it is polite,
if not vital, to write to these people, explaining who you are, what
you are doing and asking if they would mind you visiting them.
This is infinitely preferable to turning up on someone's doorstep,
announcing, 'I'm a friend of your uncle's cousin twice removed—
can you put me up?'

Making contacts while you are abroad involves patience, understanding, and respect for your surroundings. No one likes people
who are pushy, arrogant and over-bearing and this is multiplied
ten-fold as far as travellers are concerned. But if you are fully aware
of your role as a visitor and realise that you are privileged to be
there then you will make friends quickly and find numerous doors
opening for you.

Contacts should be looked upon as a local insight into a
country—not as a means of saving money. If you are staying with
people do not over-stay your welcome, and make sure that you buy
your hosts presents and perhaps take them out for a meal.

Overcoming travel fatigue

One of the great benefits of having people to stay with is that it
gives you a chance to put your feet up, empty your bags and take
stock of what you have been doing. This is a vital part of travelling
over a period of several months—if you are on the move continually
then your senses eventually become dulled to the sights and sounds
around you. Most people agree that three months of continuous
travelling is more than enough before travel fatigue sets in. At this
point, no matter how glorious the sunset is or how magnificent the
temple, you merely nod and move on to the next sight.

Even if you do not have contacts with whom to stay, make sure
that from time to time you spend at least a few weeks in one place
so that you can put your activities into perspective.

USING UNUSUAL MODES OF TRANSPORT

During your year abroad you will be able to travel on more forms
of transport than you thought imaginable as you sat on the Number
7 bus or the London Underground. Travelling on public transport

systems abroad can be an experience in itself, as anyone who has stepped foot on a bus in Pakistan can testify, but it is worthwhile looking for alternative forms of transport.

While Ian Dennis, a student from Durham, was in Kenya he was faced with the prospect of an arduous trip from Malindi, an island off the north coast, to the southern town of Mombasa:

'I had reached Malindi after a five-hour bus trip, during which time I spent more time in mid-air than on my seat. This was followed by a ride in a tiny ferry that was so over-crowded that the sides were barely above the waterline. After three weeks on Malindi I was not relishing the prospect of a return journey, when a small, bearded man asked me if I wanted to take a dhow back to Mombasa. I jumped at the chance and spent three idyllic days (including one when we were becalmed) lying on a dhow that was totally devoid of any metal parts—an engine was out of the question. I spent the days fishing and talking to the crew members. At night I was lulled to sleep by the lapping of the water against the side of the dhow, as I watched shooting stars (or maybe satellites) flash across the sky overhead. Infinitely preferable to an airborne bus.'

Other possible forms of transport include:

- Kyaks and inflatable rafts
- Horses, camels and yaks
- Hot-air balloons
- Motorised rickshaws
- Microlights
- Lorries

EXPERIENCING THE THRILL OF DANGER

You only have to turn on the television to discover that there are wars going on all over the world. Many people would go to great extremes to avoid these areas. However, two groups sometimes actively seek them—newspaper foreign correspondents and independent travellers. For the newspaper men it is a vocation, so what excuse can travellers offer? Much of it has to do with testing yourself in situations that you have never encountered before, as New Zealand traveller Marcus Adams explains:

'While travelling overland through southern Africa I had the choice of going by train through Zambia or taking an armed convoy through Mozambique, where a debilitating civil war had been raging for several years. I chose the Mozambique route, nicknamed the Gun Run, for the simple reason that I have had a reasonably comfortable, middle-class life and I wanted to see what it would be like to be in a life-threatening situation.

'The Gun Run consists of 40 to 50 trucks which drive through northern Mozambique. They are escorted by armoured vehicles from the Zimbabwe army, whose presence is intended to deter the Renamo guerillas from attacking the convoy. This is not always successful and every week lorries are attacked by snipers, or blown up by landmines. As it was, the lorry in which I rode had a bullet hole in the windscreen and the driver kept looking around the hills nervously. On this occasion there were no attacks on the convoy and I reached Zimbabwe after eight of the most exhilarating hours of my life.'

Even if you do have a thirst for danger it is wise to take a few precautions:

- Keep the risks reasonable—don't try to penetrate war zones.
- Never do anything the locals would not do.
- Never try to go anywhere that is classed as off-limits, either by the Foreign Office in Britain, or by the local authorities.
- Always tell someone at home what your intended travel plans are.
- Always remain as unobtrusive as possible while in politically or military sensitive areas.
- If you are faced with gunfire—keep your head down.
- Beware even when the fighting has stopped—landmines and booby-traps are frequently left as the legacy of war. In Afghanistan it is estimated that there are over ten million unexploded landmines.

MAKING THE MOST OF YOUR MONEY

Travelling can often be very economical—a lot cheaper than everyday living at home, as Tammi Dallaston Wood found when she was travelling in India:

'The vast proportion of your money is apportioned to costs of accommodation and food, so if you find yourself strapped for cash, these are the areas you should economise on. Try eating at roadside stalls, always ensuring that the food is piping hot (temperature, not spices—you can be guaranteed of that!). Most beach resorts are okay to sleep out on (Konark, Orissa, Goa, Om Beach, Karnataka). Hire a room with a group of friends (you'll find them!), dump your gear and bed down in the sand. Before sleeping out in the open, seek local advice about snakes, poisonous insects, dogs, monkeys and any other dangerous animals, including the human variety. In places where there are a lot of western tourists (Puri, Orissa, Pushkar, Rajasthan, Tamil Nadu) you can try to obtain waitressing/cooking/dogsbody work in return for board and/or food.

'I was in India for six months, travelled through every state bar Kashmir (too dangerous) and spent only £550. A fellow traveller came overland to India through Turkey, Iran and Pakistan and she spent £600 in eight months.

MAKING FLEXIBLE TRAVEL PLANS

Although it is important to do your homework before you go it is possible to be over-prepared. When Sydneysider Laura Hasler was planning her world tour her father prepared a schedule that detailed her movements on an almost daily basis:

'At first I thought this was a good idea because it meant that I would always know what I was doing. But after a couple of weeks I realised it was restrictive beyond belief and I began to feel I was travelling in a strait-jacket. I eventually tore it up and then I began to enjoy myself—relying more on my instincts and being able to react to situations as they happened around me.'

Flexibility is the by-word of the traveller, and one of the joys of travel is that plans are constantly changing as you meet different people and hear of new places to visit. With this in mind it is advisable to avoid the temptation of buying an around-the-world plane ticket. These are excellent value and in some case a tremendous buy. However, they can be slightly restrictive, and unless you are sure you will be visiting a number of particular countries and cities it is perhaps a better idea to buy a one-way ticket and see how your plans develop from there (see Chapter Seven).

Treat yourself

Most long-term travellers work to a reasonably tight budget but there are times when even the most hardened voyager can benefit from a little luxury. A slap-up meal or a night in a high-class hotel can do wonders for recharging the batteries. It may seem expensive at the time but it is well worth it and should be looked at as an investment for the rest of your trip.

GOLDEN RULES OF TRAVEL

- Do some research about the places you are going to visit.
- Respect the people and places you visit.
- Take time to get to know a place in depth.
- Use your initiative and do not always follow the crowd.
- Keep an open mind about changing your travel plans.
- Enjoy yourself.

THE GOOD TRAVELLER'S QUIZ

1. You are faced with an over-loaded bus in a Third World country. Do you:
   a March on, remind people about the Empire and demand a seat?
   b Sit on the floor and befriend the nearest goat?
   c Decide to take the train instead?

2. You are approached by someone offering you a lift on his camel. However, you think he looks distinctly shifty. Do you:
   a Tell him that camels give you the hump?
   b Ask around to see if anyone else knows about this?
   c Report him to the nearest policeman?

3. You meet a touring rugby team from your home town. Do you?
   a Join them in drinking games and reminisce about how wonderful life is at home?
   b Ask them if they have been anywhere that is worth a visit?
   c Ignore them and pretend you don't speak English?

4. Your guidebook states that a certain hotel is wonderful, but it turns out to be a dump. Do you:
   a Write a vitriolic letter to the publishers threatening to sue them for every penny they have?
   b Write to the publishers pointing out that perhaps the hotel has changed hands?
   c Throw away your guidebook?

5. A friend of a friend invites you to stay with them for as long as you like. Do you:

a   Take them up on it and stay for six months?
b   Stay for a week, buy them a small gift and invite them to visit you in Britain?
c   Feel uneasy about imposing on them?

6. A border guard demands a bribe when you enter a country. Do you:
a   Storm off in a huff, calling him a dictator?
b   Pay up and put it down to experience?
c   Pay up grudgingly and feel as if you have been conned?

7. You reach a place where you planned to stay a month but soon discover that you do not like it. Do you:
a   Stay a month anyway out of stubborness?
b   Wait a week and if it does not improve move on?
c   Formulate a new plan immediately?

8. Your bus breaks down in the middle of nowhere. Do you?
a   Curl up and die?
b   Follow what the locals do?
c   Ask if anyone is a member of the AA?

Your score
Mostly a. Hopeless! You could be in line for the World's Worst Traveller Award. You should reassess your attitude quickly if you want to avoid being thrown in front of an oncoming train.
Mostly b. You have a good attitude for travelling and you should go far. You have the right amount of inquisitiveness but you are also sensitive to your surroundings and the feelings of others.
Mostly c. You have the potential to be a good traveller but you should relax more and become more aware of the people and places around you.

7
Getting There and Beyond

Your first task as a traveller is deciding how to get to your destination. Short of crossing the Atlantic in a barrel or flying over Europe in a hot-air balloon, you will have to choose between:

- air
- rail
- sea
- road

GOING BY AIR

Arguably the most uncomfortable form of travel ever invented but undoubtedly the quickest. If you want to go immediately from Britain to your destination then you should look around for the cheapest flights available.

Airline seats, like every other commodity, are sold at a variety of prices for the same item and it is important to shop around for the best offers.

Bucket shops

In the 1970s 'bucket shops'—named after dubious activities on the US stock market in the 19th century—appeared in Britain, selling illegally discounted airline tickets. Although it is still theoretically against the law to sell discounted tickets in this way no action is ever taken by the government and it has become an accepted part of airline ticket sales.

Most bucket shops are located in London and they advertise regularly in the national press as well as *City Limits, TNT, Time Out* and the *Standard*. Although there is still a slight stigma of doubt attached to bucket shops the vast majority of them are highly reliable. But if you are booking a ticket through them make sure thay are a member of the **Association of British Travel Agents** (ABTA), or licensed by the **International Air Transport Association** (IATA). An additional safeguard of reliability is if they accept Access or Visa—these companies check their credibility very carefully before dealing with them.

The **Air Travel Advisory Bureau** (Tel: (0171) 636 5000) will provide you with telephone numbers of reputable bucket shops dealing with your desired destination.

High street travel agents

Since the appearance of bucket shops the major travel agents have cottoned on to the importance of discounted tickets. They now all offer various discounts on 'flight only' tickets, but they will invariably be higher than the bucket shops. Sometimes travel agents will quote you the first price that comes up on their computer. In some cases there will be others seats at lower prices so it is worth asking if this is the only price available.

For many people the advantage of a local travel agent outweighs the lower prices of the London bucket shops.

Types of ticket

First Class

Outside the reach of the independent traveller, but if you are ever offered the chance to travel First Class, take it up—it will totally change your views on air travel.

Apex/Super Apex (Advance Purchase Excursion)

One of the best options for the traveller looking for the best deal. It is the method whereby airlines offer officially discounted seats. There are certain restrictions with APEX tickets—they must be booked and paid for well in advance of departure, varying between seven days and a month, a minimum stay abroad is required and there are no stopovers allowed. However, these are minor considerations for the committed traveller with a relatively flexible agenda. They are well worth the reductions of up to 60 per cent.

Pex/Super Pex (Public excursion fare)

Similar to Apex except that there is no advance-purchase requirement. Thirty per cent cancellation fee.

Excursion fares
Available on some long-haul routes and with fewer restrictions
than Apex. Flights can be changed and the savings on full economy
fares are between 25 and 30 per cent.

Standby fares
Cheap seats on the day of departure—available mainly on routes
to North America. Although the tickets can be bought three
months before departure, it will depend on the availability on the
day. A reasonable option if you can wait around until a seat
becomes available.

Round-the-world tickets (RTW)
The cheapest way to fly around the world, with prices starting
from £695. Most of them are valid for a year and you have to make
a minimum of at least three stopovers. Although they are great
value you should think carefully before you choose this form of
ticket. You will have to keep travelling in the same direction and
you will not be allowed to 'backtrack'. Ask yourself if you really
do want to visit all the destinations on your ticket or if you are
going just because it is a cheap option. They tend to remove
flexibility from the independent traveller.
   Companies specialising in RTW tickets include:

Trailfinders Ltd
   42–50 Earls Court Road   194 Kensington High Street
   London W8 6FT   London W8 7RG
   Tel: (0171) 938 3366   Tel: (0171) 938 3939
   (Long-haul)   (Long-haul)

   58 Deansgate   215 Kensington High Street
   Manchester M3 2FF.   London W8 6BD
   Tel: (0161) 839 6969   Tel: (0171) 937 5400
                                     (Transatlantic and European)

   48 Corn Street   22–24 The Priory Queensway
   Bristol BS1 1HQ   Birmingham B4 6BS
   Tel: (0117) 929 9000   Tel: (0121) 236 1234

   254-284 Sauchiehall Street
   Glasgow G2 3EH
   Tel: (0141) 353 2224

STA
  86 Old Brompton Road
  London SW7 3LH
  Tel: (0171) 937 9962
Also offices throughout the country including Manchester,
Glasgow, Leeds, Oxford, Cambridge, Bristol and Brighton

  A good investment is also the *Round the World Air Guide* by
Katie Wood and George McDonald (Fontana).

Airlines

Airlines around the world vary in terms of service, punctuality and
flight times. For most independent travellers cost will be the main
consideration and in this regard you should not be afraid to use
less well-known airlines, such as some of the eastern European and
Asian carriers. Particularly if it is one-off then the low price will
be well worth the few moments of discomfort you may experience.
However, you may dispute this if you have just spent 40 hours,
including numerous delays, getting to Australia.

Safety

As the lead character in the film *Rain Man* pointed out, QANTAS
is the only airline that has never crashed. Safety is always a
consideration when flying but in reality it is one of the less
dangerous forms of travel. Certain South American airlines have
poor safety records and, in general, internal flights are more prone
to accidents than international ones.

Air couriers

A few years ago it was possible to obtain flights for next to nothing
by acting as a casual air courier—taking important packages by
hand to foreign countries. However, in recent years there has been
such an increase in the number of people offering their services
that the courier companies are now charging considerable fees. In
most cases you are required to return within 28 days of your
outward flight and some companies ask for a sizeable deposit to
make sure that you do not disappear into the sunset. However, it
is a good way to spend a few weeks in places as far afield as Harare
and Auckland*.

*Courier companies come and go with alarming regularity so it might be a good
idea to have a look at a London Yellow Pages in your local library.

Ticketing
- Ensure you confirm your ticket at least 72 hours before your departure date. This applies wherever you are flying from in the world.

- Ensure that your ticket has OK in the 'Status' box. This means the ticket has been confirmed. If the letters RQ appear then it means the flight has been requested but not confirmed. WL means you have been 'wait-listed'. OPEN indicates you have not yet decided when you want to travel.

- In Third World countries make sure you buy your ticket in person, not over the phone. Check and re-check your ticket: in some countries where there is no computerised system there is a tendency to over-book flights.

What are the pros of air travel?
- Quick—you can be in a foreign country in the time it would take to cross London in the rush-hour.

- Value for money—if you are prepared to be discriminating in your choices.

- Relatively safe—in 1990 air passengers worldwide made 1.3 billion flights. During that period there were 300 deaths in 12 jet airliner accidents. This means, on average, you would have to make 4.3 million flights before a fatality occurred. Compare this with the fact that in Britain, in 1990, 5000 people died in motoring accidents.

And the cons?
- Uncomfortable—unless you can afford the luxury of flying First or Business Class, then aircraft seats are among some of the smallest ever designed. And as for the food . . .

- Disconcerting—being transported from Britain to somewhere on the other side of the world in a matter of hours can be unsettling both physically and emotionally. Time must be taken to overcome this almost instantaneous change.

- Loss of luggage—backpacks and suitcases have an unfortunate propensity for becoming detached from their owners during air travel. Although they are frequently reunited it is a good idea to carry all your valuables in your hand luggage.

GOING BY RAIL

Many travellers consider the train to be the ultimate form of travel, looking at it as an experience in itself as well as a means of getting from A to B. This may not be the case if you have to commute to work by train but for someone with time to spend it is one of the most exhilarating ways to get around. You only have to read Paul Theroux's *The Great Railway Bazaar* to be persuaded about the merits of rail travel.

Europe
Getting around Europe by train can be a relatively expensive operation, particularly when compared to the price of rail travel in Third World countries. However, for the under 26s there are two methods of lowering the cost:

- **Eurotrain tickets**. These are for use on specific routes, so if you have one destination in mind they are good value. They offer up to 50 per cent discounts and can be purchased at 52 Grosvenor Gardens, London SW1W 0AG. Tel: (0171) 730 3402, or from branches of Campus Travel.

- **Inter-Rail cards**. These are now calculated according to the number of zones visited in Europe: for the under 26s one zone is £185 for 15 days, £220 for two zones for a month, £245 for three zones and £275 for four zones. This entitles the holder to a month's travel within the designated zones, discounted travel in the UK, and reduction on certain ferry routes. You can buy Inter-Rail cards from all main line British Rail stations and British Rail appointed travel agencies. You will need two passport-size photographs and proof that you are under 26 at the time of purchase. Great value for a short-term trip, or even travelling through Europe and then continuing with your journey after a month.

- **Inter-Rail 26+**. Similar to Inter-Rail but for the over-26s. £275 for one month.

The over 60s are also catered for:

- **Rail Europ Senior Cards** can be bought by holders of a British Rail Senior Citizen Card (£16) for £5. These are valid for a year and offer reductions of up to 30 per cent in Western Europe.

Going further afield

For the long-term traveller it is once you leave Europe that rail travel really comes into its own. At times it may be over-crowded, infuriatingly slow, and unhygienic—but it is ultimately one of the greatest experiences you will have during a year abroad. The thing to remember is that you will have to shed all your previous notions about travelling by train.

Ticketing

When buying a train ticket in most Third World countries (where rail travel is extremely cheap and therefore used widely) you will need initiative, patience and at times physical strength. Queuing takes place in something akin to an expanded rugby scrum and you may have to visit several ticket offices before you achieve your objective. Don't be afraid to use your elbows, otherwise you may never reach the ticket office. Even so, expect to spend at least two hours buying a ticket in a busy station.

It is a good idea to enlist local help when trying to buy rail tickets in countries like Peru, China and India. There is a strict procedure to follow and without local knowledge you may be totally lost. For instance, the task of getting a rail ticket in China is one that is akin to completing an army assault course blindfolded.

At smaller stations the hardest thing is sometimes galvanising the station master, as one traveller in Pakistan explains:

'After visiting the ancient ruins of Moenjodaro I had six hours to wait at the local station for the next train to Lahore. This did not stop the station master sleeping the day away instead of issuing me with a ticket. When I did eventually get it the train was already pulling out of the station. As I ran after it, dozens of people on the roof (they are standard issue on Pakistan trains) cheered me on board.'

Timetabling
Dar es-Salaam, in Tanzania, has one of the most impressive-looking stations in Africa. Unfortunately, it only has three or four trains leaving it every week. Because of this the best way to find out when the train is leaving is to go to the station and ask at the ticket office. In general, verbal information is preferable to written timetables, which can be hopelessly out of date. Make sure you ask a number of people—officials as well as fellow travellers.

Always try to get to the station well in advance of the departure time. This not only safeguards you against the possibility of the train leaving early but it will give you a chance to get ahead of the crowds that will be trying to cram themselves onto the train when it arrives.

Should I travel first, second or third class?
Choosing which class to travel is a major consideration. Due to the low prices first class will be in reach of almost every traveller and on occasions this should be tried just for a little luxury. Even second class is of a high standard, particularly in ex-colonial countries where the old rolling stock is still in use. In Kenya, for example, second class compartments have your own name on the outside of the carriage, and beds and washing facilities inside. The dining car provides good quality food, served by waiters in white, starched jackets.

Third class is invariably very cheap, very crowded and can test the patience of even the most even-tempered traveller. Unless you are very hard-up you may prefer to keep your third class travel to a minimum.

Aspects of life
The great joy of rail travel is the people you meet, the sights you see and the feeling that you are moving through an area at a pace that is conducive to absorbing your surroundings. In countries such as India, the accepted Mecca of rail travel, you will see, hear and feel all aspects of humanity; from the teeming community that is an Indian station to the chai-sellers who descend on the trains whenever they stop. You may find yourself being woken at 4am by an impromptu concert on board but join in, make the most of it and treat the train as an experience, not just a mode of transport.

The rail traveller's library
Thomas Cook's Overseas Timetable
  Thomas Cook Publications
  PO Box 36
  Thorpe Wood
  Peterborough PE3 6SB
or
BAS Overseas Publications
  45 Sheen Lane
  London SW14 8LP
Indispensable for the serious rail traveller outside Europe. (Also includes road and shipping services.)

Thomas Cook's European Timetable, as above.

Newman's Indian Bradshaw. Covers every passenger train on the 35,000 miles of India's rail network.

Classic railway journeys
There are several glamorous, and expensive, tours available around the world but sometimes the ordinary passenger trains are better value for money:

● The Trans-Siberian Express. Desolate, but a must for the enthusiast.
● The Indian-Pacific. Sydney to Perth, across the Nullabor desert.
● Central Railway of Peru. Rises to 15,500 feet above sea level, the highest point in the world reached by a passenger train. Oxygen masks available on request.
● Nairobi to Mombasa. Short but sweet. Travel at day to catch a view of the game at the side of the track.
● Anywhere in India.

What are the pros of rail travel?
● cheap if you travel on the right trains in the right countries;
● easy pace of travel;
● good way to meet people.

And the cons?
● buying tickets can be a hassle;

- possibility of theft of luggage;
- can be frustratingly slow if you are in a hurry. (There are exceptions to this of course, most notably in Japan.)

GOING BY SEA

Commercial shipping

Unfortunately for the intrepid voyager, the days of working a passage on commercial shipping sailing under a British flag have all but passed. Union and nautical regulations mean that unless you are a registered seafarer (ie a qualified Merchant Seaperson) you will not find casual employment and a ride over the ocean waves with a British registered ship.

However, all is not lost. Various nations do still allow their shipping lines to take on unqualified, casual workers. These include ships flying the flags of Panama, Liberia, Liechtenstein and several Far East countries. This may not be ideal for transport from Britain but it could be utilised once you are in other parts of the world. Cargo vessels go regularly between the Americas and the Antipodes and employment is available occasionally. A direct approach is best: find the captain of a commercial ship (medium sized cargo ships are best) and ask him if he requires any working passengers.

If you do obtain a job on a commercial line you will work long hours and do all the dirty jobs going. You will need to have full travel insurance for the duration of the voyage, a visa for the country you are heading to, a certificate of good health including proof of relevant inoculations and a cash bond of approximately £200.

One company that has taken on working passengers in the past is:

Columbus Maritime Services
  Ost-West Strasse 59
  2000 Hamburg 11
  Germany

Freighter

One way of travelling by ship is to pay for a cabin on a freighter. Despite the fact that this is an expensive way to travel it is proving increasingly popular, particularly with the over 60s, and some companies have long waiting lists. For the independent traveller with limited means it may not be the most practical mode of transport.

A list of companies carrying passengers, and all other matters nautical, can be found in:

ABC Passenger Shipping Guide
ABC International
Church Street
Dunstable
Bedfordshire
Tel: (01582) 600111

Yachting
Travelling on a private yacht is a definite possibility if you are in the right area. Yachtsmen and women are not subject to the same strict regulations as commercial shipping and they can, and do, take on passengers cum general dogsbodies. This may involve painting the deck while sailing through the South Sea islands or keeping watch on a voyage to the Caribbean—wherever there are yachts on the water there will be people looking for crew. Because of this it is best to make some simple preparations before you commit yourself to a trip under sail:

1. Find out if you actually enjoy sailing. If you do not have much experience get some before you go. Find the nearest yachting club to you and ask if you can join them for a day or two.

2. Undertake some basic nautical training: learn how to tie a sheep-shank, know your port from your starboard and familiarise yourself with the various shipping signs and terminology. Even with this rudimentary information you will be an asset to the skipper of a yacht rather than a mere passenger.

3. Take a short sailing course. This is not essential but could be invaluable to you. **The Royal Yachting Association**, Romsey Road, Eastleigh, Hampshire SO5 4YA, offer courses at their centres around the country. The grade of Competent Crew can be reached in approximately a week and costs in the region of £220.

4. Buy suitable waterproofs.

With this preparation you can feel reasonably confident of finding a yacht skipper somewhere in the world to take you on. You can either do this by looking for 'Crew wanted' notices in 'yachtie' areas or else there are various organisations which specialise in finding crew for yachts:

Cruising Association
  CA House
  1 Northey Street
  Limehouse Basin
  London E14 8BT
  Tel: (0171) 537 2828
£18 registration fee.

Crewit
  Shute Hill Cottage
  Malborough
  Kingsbridge
  Devon TQ7 3SG
  Tel: (01548) 561897

£30 registration fee but for this you receive a high quality service that provides crew to and from anywhere in the world.

What are the pros of travel by sea?
- An entirely new environment compared with travel on firm ground.
- Opportunities for casual employment on private boats.
- A challenging way to travel—you will learn a lot more than if you were sitting on a plane for a few hours.
- A wide range of 'characters' inhabit the seafaring world.

And the cons?
- Slow and occasionally erratic form of transport.
- There is nowhere to hide on a ship or a yacht if you do not get on with your fellow crew members.
- Single women should be very careful because sometimes they are taken on as crew for all the wrong reasons. Establish the ground rules before accepting an offer of a place on board.

- Piracy is a very real threat in some parts of the world, most particularly the South China Sea and, increasingly, areas of the Caribbean.
- Seasickness is one of the worst feelings known to mankind.

GOING BY ROAD

For the traveller who is keen on motorised transport by road there are three options:

- coach
- conventional car
- overland vehicle

By coach

If you are looking for a cheap way to get from Britain to the continent then a long distance coach is a definite possibility. There are several companies which specialise in this including:

Eurolines
  23 Crowley Road
  Luton
  Bedfordshire LU1 1HX
  Tel: (01582) 404511

Campus Travel
  52 Grosvenor Gardens
  London SW1W 0AG
  Tel: (0171) 730 3402

Pros
- cheap;
- plenty of time to read, socialise and contemplate your destination;
- you can get the feel of countries as you are travelling through them.

Cons
- cramped—wear loose-fitting clothing;
- infrequent stops so take plenty of food;
- can take longer going through customs;

- on air-conditioned coaches it can get quite cold at night—have access to warm clothing and a blanket if possible.

By car
Some people swear by the joys of having a car abroad, others would not touch it with a ten-foot dipstick. As a rule, if you are not a driving enthusiast when you are at home then it is not a good time to start when you go abroad.

If you are a confirmed motor-addict then you could take a car from Britain. However, this is perhaps not the best idea unless you are driving to Europe. A better plan, particularly if you are in North America or the Antipodes, is to buy a car when you get there. This can be done relatively cheaply and once you have finished your travels you can sell it and recoup some of your money. One of the great advantages of this is that you can arrange technicalities like insurance and tax on a local basis and not worry about the problems of crossing borders and the red-tape that this entails.

Overland companies
A number of companies, such as Encounter Overland, Guerba and Exodus Expeditions, specialise in long-haul overland expeditions. These usually take place in converted Bedford trucks and the most popular routes are through Africa and Asia. These tours normally take several weeks and visas and injections are organised for you. Food is bought through a kitty system and cooked by one of the employees of the tour company.

Pros
- Experienced staff who know all the best areas to visit and some of the dodges to make life run more smoothly.
- You get the benefits of an organised tour while still retaining the rough edges that distinguish the traveller from the tourist.
- A happy band of travelling companions—hopefully!

Cons
- You will be travelling in cramped conditions with at least a dozen other people. If you fall out with any of them there is nowhere to hide. Some travellers have been known to 'jump truck' halfway through these tours and make their own way.

- It is a relatively expensive way to travel through these countries.
- You have to go where the truck takes you.

Overland on your own

Only the experienced off-road driver should consider an overland journey by car. Even if you have been driving in Britain for a long time this does not necessarily mean you could jump into a Land Rover and drive across the Sahara: some people are horrified by driving standards on the Continent but overland driving is an expedition rather than a Sunday afternoon outing.

If you do have an adventurous, motorised spirit you will have to buy a suitable vehicle. Your best bet would be a short-wheelbase Land Rover, Toyota Land Cruiser or a Land Rover Discovery. You will need to fill this with virtually every spare part imaginable and enough provisions for *twice* the length of your proposed trip.

An overland journey is not for the novice and even for the experienced off-road driver expert advice should be sought before leaving. The two most important things to remember are:

1. Make sure you have enough drinking water.
2. Never leave your vehicle if you break down.

For more detailed information on off-road driving consult Chapter 5 of *The Traveller's Handbook* (WEXAS).

USING LOCAL TRANSPORT

Once you get to your destination one of the best methods of getting around is local transport. This usually means buses, which are a wonderful way of meeting people (sometimes because they are sitting on your lap), getting around for next to nothing, and seeing a country as its inhabitants see it. However, a word of warning: newspapers in Third World countries frequently have headlines declaring 'Bus crashes into ravine—34 killed, 76 injured.' This highlights the fact that it is not necessarily the safest form of transport and also that these vehicles tend to be slightly overloaded.

There is no way of assessing the safety potential of local buses—most of the vehicles are at least 20 years old and the drivers seem to have invariably been trained by Damon Hill. It is one

instance of taking your life in your hands and hoping that it will
not be you making the headlines the next morning.

As for catching local buses, the best idea is to rely on local
knowledge. Always check with the driver that the bus is going to
the desired destination. Luggage is frequently stored on the roof
so make sure that you have all your valuables about your person.

Other forms of local transport that should be used if possible
are:

- Converted mini-buses. These have different names in different
  countries and operate in cities and also further afield. There
  is a constant competition to see how many people can be
  crammed into these vehicles so do not be surprised if you find
  yourself on the outside of the back door, hanging on for dear
  life.

- Rickshaws. These are generally bicycle-powered or motorised
  these days.

- Tuk-tuks. A large, covered seat with a motorbike attached.
  Not good for the life expectancy.

- Ferries. Tend to be grossly overloaded too.

- Tongas. Down-to-earth, horse-drawn carriages.

PREPARING TO HITCHHIKE

Most people will turn to hitchhiking at some stage of their time
abroad. In developed countries it is best to look clean and fresh
(even if you do not feel it), hitch in small numbers (but preferably
not alone), stay away from other hitchers, and do not hitch in towns
as the police may take a dim view of this.

In Third World countries hitching is a slightly different ball-
game. Motor vehicles are often at a premium and it is a much more
accepted fashion of general transport than in the West. In some
countries, such as El Salvador where the public transport system
has virtually disappeared, it has all but replaced the public buses
and equivalent fares are expected from hitchers. This is true for
most Third World countries—do not be surprised, or offended, if
you are asked for money for your lift. This is just the accepted

norm and the price will probably be nominal—but make sure you agree on it before you get in.

Although there are some horror stories about hitching the risks can be lessened greatly:

Don't   — accept a life from anyone who is obviously drunk or high on drugs;
         — hitch after dark;
         — hitch alone if you are a woman—unfortunately this is a problem all over the world.

Do   — find out the correct hitching sign for the country you are in;
         — offer to pay for a lift if this is expected;
         — be wary of any offers of accommodation. But do not be afraid to accept if they seem genuine.

8
What Should I Take?

OFFICIAL DOCUMENTS

There are two things that you *must* take with you when you travel
overseas:

- passport
- insurance

For many other countries the list will also include:

- visas
- vaccination certificates

Although you will be guarding your official documents with
every fibre of your being while you are abroad, it is a good idea to
leave a copy of each one at home. Either make photocopies of the
relevant parts or else write down all the necessary information such
as passport numbers, insurance policy dates and the date and place
of issue of vaccination certificates. Leave these in the hands of
someone responsible who will be able to relay them to you if
necessary.

OBTAINING A PASSPORT

Everyone knows you need a passport to travel overseas but it is
surprising how many people leave it to the last minute to apply for
one, or suddenly realise that it will run out halfway through their
trip. Even if your passport is valid until after your proposed date
of return it may be necessary to apply for a new one: some
countries, including Australia and Thailand, require a passport to

be valid for a period of time beyond the length of your intended stay. This varies from three to six months, but to be on the safe side it is best to have twelve months leeway just to prevent any unnecessary hassle.

Another unforeseen problem with passports can be space. The standard 32-page ones can fill up with alarming alacrity if you are moving through several stamp-happy countries. If your passport does become full you may be refused entry at your next port of call. This can be overcome by applying for a 48-page passport. These cost £27 as opposed to £18 for the regular ones of 32 pages, but they are worth considering if you hope to be taking in several countries. Both types are valid for ten years.

It is a good idea to memorise your passport number—it will save you a lot of time while filling in visa forms and the such like.

Will I need two passports?
Certain countries will not grant you entry if you have particular stamps in your passport. In the past this has applied specifically to stamps from Israel and South Africa. With the easing of the political situation in the latter this will soon cease to be a problem, but you may still like to ask for a detachable piece of paper in your passport on which they can put the stamp. If you are visiting Israel and then planning to go to Arab countries it would be a good idea to get a second passport. Again, this situation is easing, but immigration officers are not always renowned for their glasnost.

London Passport Office
  Clive House
  70 Petty France
  London SW1H 9HD
  Tel: (0171) 279 3434
  Personal callers only—
  urgent cases

Liverpool Passport Office
  5th Floor
  India Buildings
  Water Street
  Liverpool L2 0QZ
  Tel: (0151) 237 3010

Newport Passport Office
  Olympia House
  Upper Dock Street
  Newport
  Gwent NP9 1XA
  Tel: (01633) 244500

Peterborough Passport Office
  Aragon Court
  Northminster Road
  Peterborough PE1 1QC
  Tel: (01733) 895555

Glasgow Passport Office
  3 Northgate
  96 Milton Street
  Cowcaddens
  Glasgow G4 0BT
  Tel: (0141) 332 0271

Belfast Passport Office
  Hampton House
  47-53 High Street
  Belfast BT1 2QS
  Tel: (01232) 232371

Application forms can be obtained from the Post Office and most travel agents.

Checklist
1. Apply for your passport in good time—months, rather than weeks, before your departure. Processing of your application will take longer over Christmas and the height of summer.
2. Make sure your passport is valid for a minimum of six months *after* the date you plan to return to the UK.
3. Ensure that you have enough spare pages for the number of countries you expect to visit.
4. Make sure you know where your passport is at all times.
5. Never give your passport to anyone else.

GETTING VISAS

Visas are the magic stamps in your passport which allow you to enter and leave foreign countries. Although you do not need them for EEC member states (and in some instances the USA and certain Eastern Bloc countries) you will for most other countries. Visas invariably cost money so you will have to include this in your travel budget.

What type of visa?
- **Tourist**—you can enter a country once, for a specified period.

- **Re-entry**—you can go back to a country you have already visited.

- **Multiple entry**—you can go back more than once, within a specified period of time.

Where do I get them?

In Britain visas are issued from foreign embassies. The majority of these can be contacted in London—addresses can be found in the relevant telephone book at your local library. Exceptions:

Albania
131 Rue de la Pompe
75016 Paris
France
Tel: 1-45 53 51 32

Benin
87 Avenue Victor-Hugo
75116 Paris
France
Tel: 1-45 00 98 40

Burundi
46 Square Marie Louise
1040 Brussels
Belgium
Tel: 2-230 4535

Central African Republic
29 Boulevard de
    Montmorency
75016 Paris
France
Tel: 1-42 24 42 56

Chad
65 Rue des Belles-Feuilles
75116 Paris
France
Tel: 1-45 53 36 75

Congo
37 bis
Rue Paul Valery
75016 Paris
France
Tel: 1-45 00 60 57

Djibouti
26 Rue Emile-Menier
75116 Paris
France
Tel: 1-47 27 49 22

Guatemala
73 Rue de Courcelles
75008 Paris
France
Tel: 1-47 63 90 83

Guinea
24 Rue Emile-Menier
75016 Paris
France
Tel: 1-45 56 72 25

Iran
4 Avenue d'Iena
75116 Paris
France
Tel: 1-47 23 61 22

Laos
74 Avenue Raymond-Poincare
75116 Paris, France
Tel: 1-45 53 02 98

Mali
89 Rue du Cherche-Midi
75006 Paris, France
Tel: 1-45 48 58 43

Niger
   154 Rue de Longchamp
   75116 Paris, France
   Tel: 1-45 04 80 60

Rwanda
   70 Boulevard Coucelles
   75017 Paris, France
   Tel: 1-42 27 36 31

Embassies are not only useful for obtaining visas but they should also be contacted for any general information, or restrictions.

Although it is important to have a visa for the first country you will be visiting it is not necessary to get half a dozen visas before you leave. Many travellers prefer to pick up visas en route. This has advantages and disadvantages:

The pros of getting visas en route

- Can be cheaper—particularly if you change your money on the black market.
- Gives you greater flexibility to change your plans as you go.
- You do not have to worry about delays in embassies in Britain.

And the cons

- Can be a time-consuming and frustrating business.
- Immigration officers may question you if you do not have a visa for another country—in reality this is unlikely to happen.
- If, for any reason, you are refused a visa you will have to make hasty rearrangements.

If you do apply for visas as you travel remember to take several passport-sized photographs—three dozen is not an unrealistic number

BUYING INSURANCE

This may seem like an expensive luxury, but it is not—it is an absolute necessity. If you take out insurance and do not have to use it then you should be thankful and not look at it as wasted money.

If you are planning an extended stay abroad then you should go to an insurance broker who specialises in this type of policy. There will be certain areas you will want your policy to cover:

1. **Medical Expenses**. This is the most important part of your insurance policy and you should not step foot overseas if you do not have this. The range of cover varies, but a minimum of £250,000 would be recommended while a sum of £2 million should be considered seriously, particularly if you are going to be travelling in North America where medical insurance is something of a national obsession. You may find it hard to conceive of having £1 million worth of illness, but if you break a leg in the middle of the African bush and need an air ambulance and then extensive medical treatment it is frightening how quickly the expenses mount up. Make sure your cover is total—and cross your fingers that you will never need to use it.

2. **Personal accident**. This allows for the payment of a lump sum to the policy holder in the event of an accident, such as the loss of a finger or serious disablement. The sum varies depending on the injury and most policies have set amounts. These can be increased, if desired, with an additional payment.

3. **Loss of baggage and money**. Although the independent traveller should not be weighed down by a lot of inordinately expensive items, you should be insured against the loss of your belongings and your money. Cameras are one of the most expensive items you are likely to have. If it is worth more than a couple of hundred pounds then it would be a good idea to insure it separately at home on an 'all risks' policy.

4. **Personal liability**. This insures you against sums payable if someone decides to sue you for injury, loss or damage to other people or their property. Make sure you have this because if someone decides to sue you in a country such as America they will be seeking a lot more money than the price of a hot-dog. Personal liability does not cover third party motor insurance.

5. **Cancellation**. If the policy holder has to cancel a journey for a genuine reason such as ill health then any money already paid as a deposit will be insured.

6. **Strikes and delays**. This will mean you are compensated if your journey (from Britain) is delayed or effected by a strike.

Making claims

If you incur heavy medical expenses you may have to pay these yourself and then claim the money from the insurance company, so make sure you can lay your hands on the money in an emergency.

If you are claiming for loss of money or baggage it is best to wait until you get home to make the claim. At the time make sure you report the loss to the local police immediately and that you receive written confirmation of this. If you lose something through negligence—such as leaving your wallet unattended on the beach while you go for a swim—the insurance company may conclude that it is your own fault and refuse to pay.

Be patient when making a claim and be prepared to have the first £25 deducted from the total.

Travel insurance specialists

Automobile Association
    Fanum House
    Basing View
    Basingstoke RG21 4EA
    Tel: (01256) 20123
Provide cover for overland travel abroad.

Campbell Irvine Ltd
    48 Earls Court Road
    Kensington
    London W8 6EJ
    Tel: (0171) 937 6981
Offer personal and vehicle insurance.

Endsleigh Insurance Services Ltd
    Endsleigh House
    Ambrose Street
    Cheltenham Spa
    Gloucester GL50 3NR
Good all-round travel insurance policies at very competitive prices.

Travel Insurance Services
    Central House
    32–66 High Street

Stratford
London E15 2PF
Tel: (0181) 522 3402

Trailfinders Travel Centre
   42–50 Earls Court Road
   London W8 6FT
Offer comprehensive cover, including up to £5 million worth of
medical insurance, for a price of up to £520 for 12 months.

Travelcare Limited
   68 High Street
   Chislehurst
   Kent BR7 5AQ
   Tel: (0800) 181532

WEXAS International
   45–49 Brompton Road
   London SW3 1DE
   Tel: (0171) 589 0500
Offer members comprehensive insurance at very competitive
prices.

For general worldwide travel insurance for a year you can expect
to pay upwards from £450 (worldwide insurance is generally more
expensive if it includes cover for North America). If you have a
policy that has been specifically tailored to your needs (for instance
you may want to travel through a war zone or be covered for
abseiling down Everest) then the premium will rise accordingly.
It is worth shopping around for the best policy for you.

Medical treatment in Europe
If you are a UK citizen travelling or working in another EC country
you are entitled to free, or greatly reduced, medical treatment. To
qualify for this you should obtain the DSS leaflet T2 *Health Advice
to Travellers* and complete form CM1 and send it, at least a month
before you are due to leave, to Department of Social Security,
Overseas Branch, Newcastle-upon-Type NE98 1YX. They will
then issue you with an E-111 (E-one-eleven) form which entitles
you to medical treatment in any EC country over a twelve-month
period. You will probably have to pay at the time, but if you make

sure you get a receipt you will be able to reclaim some, or all, of the medical costs.

Other leaflets worth getting from the DSS are: SA41 *While You're Away* and *Your Social Security Health Care and Pension Rights in the European Community.*

Summary

- Make sure you have adequate medical insurance.

- Read the small print—most policies exclude events such as 'acts of God' and the 'outbreak of civil war'. Ask for an explanation of what these terms cover.

- Check the exclusion clauses carefully—these may include an upper age limit and exclusions covering various dangerous sporting activities such as hang-gliding or skiing. Some exclusion clauses also relate to injuries sustained while working abroad. If you intend to do this you should let the insurance company know what type of work you hope to be doing. There may also be special clauses covering women who are more than seven months pregnant.

- Ask the advice of a professional insurance broker.

- Make sure your insurers know exactly what you intend to do.

- Make sure your policy is inclusive of your days of departure and return (if known).

- Find out how to extend your insurance policy if necessary.

- As with a certain credit card—Don't leave home without it.

- If you are travelling in Europe make sure that you have form E-111.

HEALTH CERTIFICATES

In many parts of Africa, Asia and South America travellers will need proof of vaccination against:

- yellow fever
- cholera

It is best to get these vaccinations as a matter of course if you are entering various Third World countries. (See Chapter 10).

Keep your vaccination certificates with you at all times, preferably held into your passport with an elastic band. If you try to enter a country which requires a certificate and you do not have one you will be given a vaccination on the spot. This can be unsafe and unhygienic—one needle is sometimes used for several injections.

SEMI-OFFICIAL DOCUMENTS

What should I take?
There are two reasons for carrying semi-official documents:

1. Helping you get a job.
2. Easing your way through customs.

As a rule of thumb take any document which you think will be useful or which looks impressive. This can include:

Copies of degrees or education certificates
These can be useful when applying for jobs, particularly in the field of Teaching English as a Foreign Language. In some countries, such as Japan, it will increase your job prospects considerably. It is a good idea to leave the original documents at home and take a photocopy with you—if it is vital to have the original then you can send for it.

Letters of introduction or sponsorship
If you have arranged to visit any organisations abroad try to get a letter of introduction. This will not only give you a contact abroad but it will show any cantankerous border guards that you have a specific goal in their country.

Plastic cards
Border guards are fascinated by small, plastic cards, particularly if they have your photograph on them. Take as many of these as you can lay your hands on, such as matriculation cards, student

discount cards (including an International Student Identity Card, which are available from student unions, and invaluable for getting travel discounts abroad), sporting association cards and the such like. One traveller who was driving through Africa was given considerable hassle by the border guards in Chad. Eventually he produced so many official-looking plastic cards that the guards relented and let him in. (Afterwards he was not sure whether they were impressed or if they just got bored with his outpouring of cards.)

Bank statements

If you can get hold of a bank statement that shows you have a significant amount of money to your name then take it with you. By the time you are overseas this sum may have evaporated but it is a useful backup. If you do not have the means for this before you go it would be worthwhile borrowing some money from a friend or relation for a short time and then get a statement immediately before you pay it back.

You may never have to use any semi-official documents but one of the joys of travel is coming across the unexpected. The better prepared you are then the better you will be able to cope with it.

CARRYING IMPORTANT DOCUMENTS

Transportation of important documents is one of the great worries for a traveller and the threat of pickpockets is constant. However, the incidences of petty theft are not as common as the stories you will hear suggest and one of the most common reasons for people losing documents such as passports is carelessness. The one golden rule is:

● Always carry important documents about your person.

The best way to do this is with:

1. A moneybelt.
2. An elasticated bandage, such as 'Tubi-grip'.

Although moneybelts are cumbersome and uncomfortable they are undoubtedly the most efficient way to carry documents. Modern-day 'bum-bags' which are of similar design but worn on the outside of the clothing, are much more prone to being pulled or cut from the wearer. If moneybelts are worn under a shirt which is tucked into trousers or a skirt it would take a very determined sneak-thief or pickpocket to deprive you of your possessions. Make sure you use a cotton moneybelt rather than a nylon one—even in mild climates they tend to get very hot and sweaty. Because of this make sure that your documents are protected against moisture. The best thing for this are small resealable plastic bags known as 'grippa-bags'.

Elasticated bandages are another way of giving pickpockets a hard time. These are bandages that are generally used for sporting injuries such as muscle strains and twists. For the traveller a large bandage for the upper thigh is invaluable—once your valuables are placed here it is extremely difficult for them to be removed against your will. This method can also be used with a bandage at the top of your arm. However, it can be uncomfortable for extended periods of time and is best used when you think you are under a serious threat of theft.

Summary

Do   — keep your valuable documents about your person at all times.
— use a moneybelt or similar implement.
— replace your documents every time they are used. This may be tiresome but it can be dangerous to become lackadaisical.
— make sure your documents are safe at night and when you are on public transport.

Don't   — carry documents in a suitcase, backpack or day-pack.
— carry documents in pockets, particularly backpockets.
— leave documents lying around in customs offices.
— post documents through the mail.

If you spend a year abroad you will be like a snail for 12 months: everything you need will be on your back so it is important to choose carefully.

CAMPING

For the experienced camper the idea of taking a tent abroad is a good option. For the novice it is a better idea to stick to the proliferation of youth hostels, lodging houses and cheap hotels which you will come across.

If you are going to camp—and bear in mind a tent is a bulky and relatively heavy item to carry around the world—you will have to look at a number of questions:

1. Are there campsites where I am going and if so where are they?
2. Will I be camping at high altitude or sea-level?
3. What type of insects/wild animals are there in the area in which I intend to camp?
4. Will I be camping all the time or only occasionally?
5. Will I be camping on my own or with others?
6. What types of weather can I expect?

The type of tent used will depend on the answers to these questions. Ultimately you will want something that is both strong and light. Three companies who specialise in a wide range of tents are:

Vango
  70 East Hamilton Street
  Ladyburn

Greenock PA15 2UB
Tel: (01475) 744122

Tarpaulin and Tent Manufacturing Company
101–103 Brixton Hill
London SW2 1AA
Tel: (0181) 674 0121

John James Hawley Ltd
Lichfield Road
Walsall WS4 2DH
Tel: (01922) 25641
They will be able to tell you the nearest stockist in your area.

BACKPACKS

The old-style, external-framed rucksacks are out; the new-style backpack-cum-carry bags are very much in. These are backpacks with conventional padded straps that can be zipped away if necessary giving the pack the appearance of a soft suitcase. They also have a zip around the entire perimeter of the bag so access is not restricted to the top. The advantages of these are enormous:

● The straps do not flap around and get caught while being transported on planes, trains and automobiles.

● They can be used as carry bags when approaching border posts, thus giving the appearance of greater respectability.

● They can fit into spaces which rigid suitcases would not.

● They can be packed and unpacked with great speed—you do not have to unpack the whole pack to get to something at the bottom.

When buying this type of pack make sure that you check three things:

1. The strength and quality of the zips. This is imperative because if a zip breaks you have no way of closing the pack.

2. Its waterproofness.
3. The straps. Make sure they are comfortable and that there is a hip strap which fastens around your waist. This will transfer 60 per cent of the weight to your legs.

The one slight disadvantage with this type of pack is that it is marginally less comfortable to carry than the current range of traditional backpacks. However, this is negligible when you consider the advantages.

When you are buying a pack resist the temptation to get the biggest one available—the bigger it is the more you will put in it. Also ensure that you can lock it. If it does not have locks on it then buy half a dozen small combination locks.

Additional bags

To save carrying a backpack around when sightseeing, going to the beach or shopping, most people take a second, smaller bag with them. This is usually in the form of:

- A daypack—a smaller version of the above type of backpack.

- A duffle bag.

- A shoulder bag.

As with the backpack make sure you can lock your bag.

Note: Thieves are constantly on the look-out for daypacks and shoulder bags to snatch, so do not carry valuables such as cameras in them.

All good camping shops, or YHA Adventure shops, will have a wide range of backpacks and daypacks. Some of the top manufacturers are:

Berghaus
   34 Dean Street
   Newcastle-upon-Tyne NE1 1PG
   Tel: (0191) 415 0200

Karrimor
   19 Avenue Parade
   Accrington
   Lancs BB5 6PR
   Tel: (01254) 385911

Vango
  70 East Hamilton Street
  Ladyburn, Greenock PA15 2UB
  Tel: (01475) 744122
It is a good investment to pay the money for a quality backpack—
it will be your companion for a long time, hopefully.

SLEEPING BAG

Even if you intend travelling in tropical countries a sleeping bag
is essential. Geography is no guarantee of temperature—Nairobi,
at 6000 feet above sea-level, can get distinctly chilly at night in the
winter. Even if you do not use a sleeping bag to sleep in all the
time it can double as a ground sheet or even a pillow.

Similarly, if you intend to stay in youth hostels or hotels you
may think that a sleeping bag is superfluous. But what of the times
you may have to sleep on public transport, at an airport, or on the
floor of a mud hut?

There are two types of sleeping bag to choose from:

- **Down**. Expensive, but excellent for cold climates. They have
  the added advantage of crushing down to a very small size. Do
  not cope well if they get wet though.
- **Synthetic**. Cheaper but not as warm. Worth considering for
  hotter climates.

The warmest type of bag is the one that is self-contained, while
the ones with zips can be used as blankets or groundsheets.

Sheet sleeping bags are useful for hot countries and for strange
hotel beds that have dirty or insect-infested sheets.

The availability of sleeping bags is as above.

BOOTS AND SHOES

These are bulky items so you will have to choose carefully and
frugally. Some of the choices are:

- High quality, leather hiking boots. If you are expecting to do
  a lot of hillwalking or trekking these would be a good investment. However, they are heavy and difficult to fit into small
  places. Make sure you break them in first—this means more

than just wearing them around the house for a few hours. Thick
socks should be worn with them. Available from camping
shops and outdoor specialists. £40 upwards.

● Lightweight, canvas walking shoes. Most travellers do a certain
amount of walking. In all but the most rugged areas this type
of shoe is ideal. They are light, dry quickly and can be squeezed
into small spaces. Available from camping shops and outdoor
specialists. £25 upwards.

● Training shoes. Also good for walking in most situations and
an asset if someone invites you for a game of squash or to run
a marathon.

● Sandals/flip-flops (thongs in Australia). Ideal for the beach
and similar situations. Also good protection when taking
showers in dirty bathrooms.

● Slippers. Some people find it comforting to take their own
slippers with them. A luxury item.

CLOTHES

Your wardrobe will depend very much on where you are going.
The important thing to remember is to take items relevant to your
destination, not your present location—when you are in windswept
Britain it is hard to imagine travelling through the scorching
Australian outback but you have to ask yourself whether you will
really need three pairs of wellies and a golf umbrella?

In both cold and hot climates it is a good idea to have loose-
fitting clothing—in cold to help trap body heat and in hot to aid
the circulation of cool air.

You will need to pack clothes for two eventualities:

1. Everyday use

Hot climates
Underwear, T-shirts, singlets, cotton trousers (jeans are not the
best type of trousers to take because they are heavy, not particularly
warm and do not dry quickly), skirts, shorts, one sweater or
sweatshirt, loose-fitting cotton shirts, swimwear.

Cold climates
Thermal underwear, fibre-pile jacket, balaclava, mittens, wool
socks.

2. Clothes for special occasions

These may be needed for visits to embassies for visas, meeting dignitaries or simply going to a posh restaurant. They should include: smart trousers or skirt, tie, sports jacket (optional) and shoes. If your smart clothes consist of black and whites you could use them if you happen to find work in a bar or restaurant.

When you are crossing borders it helps to be reasonably smartly dressed and turned out.

Should you get it there?

If you forget something you can usually buy it where you are going—there is even an illicit Marks and Spencer in northern Pakistan. This has two advantages:

1. It will probably be cheaper.
2. You will fit into your surroundings more easily if you wear clothes bought in the area.

However, this does not mean that you should rush out and kit yourself out in local dress. This may look glamorous on the locals but it tends to look pretentious and affected on visitors. Wear what feels comfortable, and respect the local customs with regard to dress. Many cultures do not like to see large expanses of bare flesh and you could cause offence if you wear shorts, singlets and swimwear in certain Muslim and African countries. Some countries have their own dress codes which have been made law: in Malawi women have to wear long skirts and it is illegal for them to wear trousers. If in doubt, dress in a conservative and respectful fashion.

What not to wear

Military-style clothing is not a good idea, particularly in politically unstable areas (this usually includes countries that have been politically unstable at any time during the last 20 years). Any khaki green or camouflaged items should be left at home.

Specialist clothing

Rohan
   30 Maryland Road
   Tongwell

Milton Keynes MK14 8HN
Tel: (01908) 216 655 (Customer Services).
And local stockists.

OTHER ITEMS TO TAKE

- Wash bag, containing soap, shampoo, toothpaste, toothbrush, shaving items (if required), sanitary towels (if required), hair brush.
- Medical bag (see Health).
- Towel: can also double as a pillow, cushion or blanket.
- Travel pillow: one of the most under-estimated traval aids known to man. Surprisingly indispensable for the independent traveller.
- Torch and batteries.
- Compass.
- Whistle.
- Toilet paper.
- Padlock.
- Maps. Make sure you buy these before you go. Some guide-books have sufficient maps.
- Guidebooks.
- Personal reading. Do not over-load yourself with reading material, but take at least one of your favourite books that you can read over and over again. Books are a good item to swap with fellow travellers.
- Writing material and notebook.
- Swiss Army knife.
- Candles.
- Small sewing kit.
- Hat: wide-brimmed for hot climates, woollen for cold.
- 'Grippa' bags: small resealable bags for keeping passports and the such like dry and clean.
- String and cord.
- Matches.
- Mosquito net.
- Mosquito coils.
- Stock of presents. These can consist of a variety of small items such as postcards, stickers, badges, biros and disposable cigarette lighters.
- Elastic bands.

- Safety pins.

Optional
- Waterproofs.
- Hair-drier. Some people cannot travel without them.
- Adaptor.
- Cassette player or Walkman.
- Dental floss—can double as string or thread in an emergency.
- Sleeping roll—can be bulky and it may be better to get used to sleeping on the ground.
- Travel iron.
- Photographs.

PACKING

Over-packing is easy to do, particularly if you follow the 'I'll take it just in case' theory of packing. You have to be practical and fairly ruthless when you are packing for a year abroad. Try following these basic steps:

1. Place all items to pack in the middle of the floor.
2. Discard everything that you are taking on the off-chance—will you really need four bottles of aftershave or perfume?
3. Get a friend to go through the pile and see if they can see any superfluous items.
4. See if it will all fit in your pack.
5. If it does not fit—return to 1.
6. If you cannot lift your pack—return to 1.
7. Continue until you have a reasonably weighted pack with which you would feel happy walking long distances if necessary.
8. Do not fill your pack to bursting—you may want to add items as you are travelling.

The schools of thought on the physical process of packing consist of the 'rollers' and the 'folders'. For no particular scientific reason the best method seems to be a combination of the two: some items of clothing are better rolled, while others, such as towels, seem to expand to an enormous size with this method and are better lain flat. However you decide to pack, experiment before you leave and find out what is best for you. As with Christmas shopping it is best not to do this at the last minute, but in reality most people do.

CHECKLIST

1. Decide if you will be camping or not.
2. Buy equipment appropriate to the areas you will be visiting.
3. Make sure your pack is lockable.
4. Make sure you have good quality zips on your pack.
5. Take a sleeping bag.
6. Take one set of smart clothing.
7. Be prepared to buy clothes when you arrive.
8. Pack with your destination in mind.
9. Do not overpack.
10. Take one or two *small* personal luxuries.

10
Staying Healthy

Being ill at home is bad enough but it can be a misery if you are travelling. There are a daunting number of weird and not-so-wonderful diseases around the world and in light of this it is sometimes surprising that we go travelling at all. However, many of these illnesses can be guarded against and others can be avoided with a little luck and some careful planning. Being aware of what could happen to you is half the battle of avoiding it.

WHAT SHOULD I DO BEFORE I GO?

There are some vaccinations that you must have before going to certain parts of the world and others that are strongly advised. Consult your GP about the relevant vaccinations for where you are going.

Required
- **Yellow fever**. Required under international health regulations for parts of Africa and South America. Valid for ten years and must be received at least ten days before entering the country concerned. Should be given separately from other vaccines. You must obtain an International Certificate for Yellow Fever and it has to be administered at specifically-designated centres. Even if a country does not have yellow fever you will need a certificate if you are coming from an infected area.

- **Cholera**. Certain countries in Africa and Asia require a certificate for this but the numbers are declining and you will not be asked for one very often. Nevertheless you should get the vaccination and a certificate. Valid for six months and should be given at least six days before departure. One injection is sufficient although two are sometimes given.

Recommended

- **Hepatitis A**. A water-borne virus that occurs mainly in the tropics, particularly in countries with poor sanitation. Immunisation is with one Gamma Globulin injection and gives up to six months protection. Some people are naturally immune to hepatitis A so arrange for a blood test first. A Gamma Globulin *does not* spread AIDS.

- **Hepatitis B**. Occurs in the tropics and countries bordering the Mediterranean. More serious than hepatitis A and is transmitted through sexual contact and contaminated blood. Immunisation usually consists of three injections but it can be expensive and is generally used for health workers and the such like. If you think you are going to an area where you are likely to be infected, for any reason, then this should be seriously considered.

- **Japanese B encephalitis**. A rare viral infection that occurs in rural areas of South East Asia and from the Indian sub-continent to Japan, Taiwan and Korea. Two injections give protection for approximately a year. Worth thinking about if you are going to be in these rural areas for prolonged periods of time.

- **Meningococcal meningitis**. Frequent epidemics in Sub-Saharan Africa, Northern India, Nepal and Saudi Arabia at the time of the Haj Pilgrimage. Epidemics do occur elsewhere (Egypt, Sudan and Kenya) and if you are travelling to a country where there is an epidemic you would be advised to get this vaccination. It takes the form of one injection that lasts for three years.

- **Poliomyelitis (polio)**. Occurs everywhere in the world and although most people in Britain will have been vaccinated against it you may need a booster. These should be every five years for travellers.

- **Rabies**. Prevalent in rural Africa, Asia and South America.

Vaccinations can be given before you go but these are generally reserved for people who will be working with animals. The best bet is to avoid contact with strange animals at all times, even domestic pets. Rabies can be transmitted to man by *any* contact of saliva with broken skin, the cornea or the lining of the nose or mouth. If you are bitten, or exposed in any other way, by an animal that you think may have rabies it is *essential* to get professional medical attention as quickly as possible as there is no known cure once the symptoms develop. You will need a course of vaccinations and possibly specific antiserum against rabies. If you have to take a considerable detour to get to suitable medical help then do not hesitate—do it.

- **Tetanus**. Occurs everywhere and travellers should ensure that they have a booster every five years.

- **Typhoid**. Transmitted through contaminated food and water and occurs everywhere except north-west Europe, North America, Australia and New Zealand. Administered in the form of two injections approximately four weeks apart. A booster is recommended every three years. A vaccination that all travellers should have.

Always consult your GP when you are travelling abroad, telling him/her all the countries you will be visiting. If you are in any doubt about your vaccination requirements contact:

Hospital for Tropical Diseases
4 St Pancras Way
London NW1 0PE
Tel: (0171) 388 9600 (Travel clinic by appointment)
or
(0839) 337733 (Pre-recorded healthline)

Liverpool School of Tropical Medicine
Pembroke Place
Liverpool L3 5QA
Tel: (0151) 708 9393 (Pre-travel advice and medical queries)
or
(0891) 172111 (Travel Health Advice—Premium (Higher) Charges apply.)

Thomas Cook Vaccination Centre
   45 Berkeley Street
   London W1X 1EB
   Tel: (0171) 499 4000
Vaccinations and certificates provided.

GETTING THERE AND ACCLIMATISATION

Jet lag
A much maligned and misunderstood concept. In medical terms
it is called the upset of your circadian (around 24 hours) or diurnal
(daytime) rhythms. To the layman this means that your body
becomes disorientated as you fly through different time zones. It
has been estimated that for every time zone you pass through you
will need one day to adjust fully. So if you pass through six time
zones it will take you six days to adapt. Westwards travel is usually
not as bad as eastwards but it can still have a marked effect.

Jet lag is a very real condition and not a figment of the travel
world's imagination. The general symptoms are:

● disorientation
● fatigue
● disrupted sleeping patterns
● disrupted eating patterns
● impaired physical and mental performance.

There is no simple solution for jet lag—except to let your body
readjust in its own time. For businessmen and the like this can be
a problem, but for travellers with more time on their hands it is
worth taking it easy for a few days and coming to terms naturally
with the change in your body time. There are weird and wonderful
inventions available to combat jet lag, such as Bioclocks which tell
you if you should be wearing sunglasses or not, but in this case
patience is definitely a virtue.

Seasickness/Motion sickness
You may get more serious illnesses while abroad but they will
probably not feel worse than with seasickness: to some people
jumping overboard would be a pleasant alternative. (This type of
sickness can also occur in cars and planes—in fact almost any form
of transport.) You can try to prevent it by:

- Remaining amidships as much as possible.
- Lying down and keeping your head still.
- Not looking at the sea—if possible keep your vision fixed on the horizon.
- Avoiding fatty foods and excessive alcohol before you travel.

If all else fails turn to the medicine cabinet. The following have shown to be effective, particularly if taken at least an hour before travel:

- Cyclizine—Marzine
- Diphenhydramine—Dramamine
- Meclozine—Bonamine, Postafine, Sealegs
- Promethazine—Avomine, Phenergan

If you suffer badly from seasickness, consult your GP before you travel.

Acclimatisation

Thanks to the wonders of air travel we can go from one extreme in climate to another in a matter of hours. This can be exhilarating for the mind—and disturbing for the body, especially if you are going from a cold climate to a hot one. During acclimatisation three main changes take place:

1. You will sweat more, at a lower temperature, and for a longer period of time.
2. Changes occur in your blood circulatory system which effects heat loss.
3. Your resting body temperature will fall.

The main result of this will be that you will lose large amounts of body salt and water. Normally this would make you thirsty and develop a taste for salt, but since your body thinks it is still back in Britain it will not necessarily send you these signals for the first few days. It is therefore very important that you drink large amounts of water (a minimum of eight pints a day) and eat extra salt. You may not feel like doing this initially but if you do not you will become dehydrated.

Various factors governing how quickly you will acclimatise are:

- Age—the young acclimatise faster.
- Fatigue—do not over-tire yourself.
- Dehydration—if you become dehydrated you will take longer to acclimatise. If your urine is a dark yellow it is a sign you are dehydrating.
- Weight—excess weight slows down acclimatisation.
- Sex—men usually acclimatise quicker than women.

Summary
- Drink at least eight pints of water a day.
- Add extra salt to your food or take salt tablets. This practice should be continued even after acclimatisation.
- Do not try and overdo it on the first few days.
- Wear loose clothing.
- Do not drink excessive amounts of alcohol—this will only hasten dehydration.
- Make sure you acclimatise properly—it can lead to other illnesses if you do not.

COMMON ILLNESSES

Diarrhoea
We have almost as many names for diarrhoea as the Eskimos have for snow (52). Call it what you will—Delhi Belly, Ho Chi Minhs or Tokyo Trots—you will almost certainly get it while you are abroad and it is very different from diarrhoea you may have had in Britain.

Diarrhoea can be caused by contaminated food or water, or it can just be the effect of a new environment, with new germs and bugs, on your system. A mild case will be irritating, with regular trips to the toilet, and a severe case will be totally debilitating— excruciating stomach cramps will be accompanied by an over-whelming, and constant, desire to go to the toilet. If you can, it is best to remain there for as long as it takes. Most cases of diarrhoea only last for three days. If the symptoms persist you may have something more serious so consult a doctor.

It is best to let diarrhoea work its way through your system, but if you *have* to travel while you have a serious case it is advisable to take some medication:

- Codeine phosphate—highly effective
- Loperamide—Imodium or Arret
- Diphenoxylate—Lomotil

Most doctors do not recommend taking anti-biotics for diarrhoea but if you are going to a very remote area you should enquire about this.

One important side-effect of diarrhoea is that you can become very dehydrated. To remedy this you should carry a sufficient supply of rehydration powders—Dioralyte or Rehidrat. These can be dissolved in drinking water and will replace lost body fluids and salts.

There are several other diseases that can be caught from contaminated food or water. These include:

- typhoid and paratyphoid
- cholera
- dysentery—bacillary or amoebic
- brucellosis—milk-borne infection

To minimise the chances of catching any of these diseases you should follow a few simple rules:

Don't   — eat in fly infested restaurants.
          — buy food or drink from street hawkers. (This is sometimes unavoidable and one of the pleasures of travelling—but you should be aware of the risks.)
          — drink anything which contains ice cubes.
          — eat food that has been cooked and left on display for a long period of time.

Do   — drink bottled water if possible.
          — boil all drinking water or milk.
          — use water purification tablets, such as Puritabs.
          — peel all fruit.
          — be wary of shellfish.
          — be wary of ice-cream.

Bilharzia (Schistosomiasis)

One of the most common diseases in many parts of Africa, Asia, the Middle East and South America. It is passed to humans through snails in any contaminated water such as lakes, ponds, reservoirs and even private swimming pools which are supplied by a local stream. Any contact with contaminted water, including swimming, wading or paddling can lead to infection. There are two strains of the disease, one of which causes blood in the urine and the other which causes blood-stained diarrhoea. It can take several months for the symptoms to develop and the best way to avoid it is not to swim in contaminated water. Even if the locals say the water is free from bilharzia you should be slightly wary and ask the advise of a doctor or local health authority. Treatment of bilharzia has improved greatly over recent years and if you think you may have been infected you should consult a centre for tropical medicine.

Malaria
Malaria is a disease which is transmitted to man by the anopheline mosquito. There are four different varieties of the disease, occurring mainly in tropical regions. There are approximately 250 million cases a year. The disease usually takes the form of a cold stage, a hot stage and profuse sweating accompanied by a fall in body temperature. The cycle takes approximately 24 hours and is repeated every other day. It can also recur several years after the initial infection. Two points to remember are:

1. It can be a killer.
2. It can be prevented.

The best way to prevent malaria is to stop mosquitoes biting you (the anopheline mosquito usually bites between dusk and dawn so this is the important time). This is easier said than done but you can take a few precautions:

- Make sure you are well covered with long trousers, or a long skirt, and a long-sleeved shirt.
- Use an effective insect repellent. Autan is recognised as one of the best, closely followed by Jungle Formula.
- Sleep under insect repellent-impregnated mosquito nets.
- Wear insect repellent-impregnated wristbands and headbands.
- Burn mosquito coils.

The other way to protect yourself is to take antimalarial drugs while you are travelling. However, due to the different strains of malaria, and the fact that some of them have become resistant to the most common antimalarial drugs, it is hard to generalise about the best courses to take.

It is currently agreed that the three most effective antimalarial drugs are:

- Proguanil
- Chloroquine
- Maloprim

These may be used in various combinations, depending on how malarious a certain area is. In many areas the malarious mosquitoes have become resistant to chloroquine.

Before you travel to a malarious country it is essential to contact your GP and ask his advice about antimalarial drugs. You will probably be given two types to take—one once a week and the other daily. It may seem an obvious point, but make sure you follow the daily and weekly doses—some travellers save them up for several days and take them all at once, and express surprise when they catch malaria. If your GP is uncertain about the latest malaria guidelines you should consult:

MASTA (The Medical Advisory Service for Travellers Abroad)
London School of Hygiene and Tropical Medicine
Keppel Street
London WC1E 7BR
Tel: (0171) 631 4408

Summary
- Find out what type of malaria exists in the area you will be visiting.
- Take expert medical advice with regard to your antimalarial drug requirements. If necessary seek a second opinion.
- Always take these as directed.
- Keep well covered in malarious areas during dusk and night.
- Use an effective insect repellent.
- Use an insecticidal spray in living areas.
- If you develop malaria seek prompt medical attention.

Other insect-borne diseases

Filariasis
Three forms, transmitted by mosquitoes, forest flies and gnats. Most at risk are agricultural workers or people on construction sites.

Kala Azar
A long-term fever which is transmitted by the tiny sandfly. Occurs mainly in areas of the southern Mediterranean. Insect repellents are essential in the battle against sandflies as they can get through mosquito-net mesh.

Sandfly fever and dengue fever
Similar to a severe case of flu. Take precautions as above.

Typanosomiasis (Sleeping sickness)
A serious illness but now limited to rural areas of west, east and southern Africa.

SUN, SNOW AND ALTITUDE

Sunburn
Not to be underestimated. In these days of decreasing ozone layers and increasing skin cancers it is important to be careful in the sun. Resist the temptation to lie in the sun for hours on end when you first reach a hot country. Fifteen to 30 minutes is more than enough time to expose yourself to the sun if you are not accustomed to it. After this, build up gradually. If you overdo it you may suffer sunstroke, causing blistering of the skin, nausea, vomiting and a severe fever. In extreme cases it can lead to death.

For those who do not like frying in the sun it is advisable to wear a wide-brimmed hat, a shirt and apply a high factor sun cream. Extra care needs to be taken when swimming and if you burn easily it is worth using a sun-block cream which should prevent any burning.

Although it is nice to have a tan, the sun should be treated with respect and some people prefer to remain 'pale and interesting'.

Prickly heat

An irritating skin rash which is caused by the blocking of the sweat glands. It is most likely to form on parts of your body where damp clothing presses against the skin, most notably the waist area, the groin, armpits, behind the knees and over the breast bone and collar bone. You can try to prevent prickly heat by:

- Wearing loose-fitting clothing;
- Avoiding man-made fibres and wearing cotton clothing;
- Washing regularly with plain water.

If you do contract prickly hear (and it is a very common condition in hot climates) try not to scratch, and apply calamine lotion or a dusting powder to the infected area, ensuring it is clean and dry first. To avoid infection Phisomed is effective as are after-shaves and body lotions.

Hypothermia

For travellers in cold climates this is a possibility. It occurs when the body temperature falls below 35 degrees centigrade and can be caused by wind, cold and wet. Acute hypothermia victims tend to act in an unpredictable manner—they are listless, surly, shivering and uncoordinated. It is a serious condition and the victims should be given immediate treatment:

- get them out of any wet clothing;
- give them shelter;
- try to warm them as quickly as possible—the best method is body-to-body contact, preferably inside a sleeping bag;
- give them hot drinks;
- do not adminster alcohol—this only lowers the body temperature.

Altitude sickness

At points over 3,500 metres (11,500 feet) some people suffer from mountain sickness due to the high altitude. This usually takes the form of headaches, fatigue, dizziness, sickness and a rapid heartbeat. If, while climbing, you feel any of these symptoms you should descend to a lower altitude and rest until you make a natural recovery. Conventional pain-killers such as paracetamol can be taken to ease the symptoms.

A more serious form of altitude sickness is **acute mountain sickness**, which can develop into the potentially fatal **high altitude pulmonary oedema** or **cerebral oedema**. The symptoms are usually puffiness around the face, blue lips, bubbly breathing and pink sputum. If anyone begins to display these symptoms it is vital that you take them to a lower altitude as quickly as possible.

AIDS AND HIV

The spread of HIV (human immunodeficiency virus) which leads to AIDS (acquired immunodeficiency syndrome) throughout the world is of particular concern to travellers. HIV is contracted through:

- Sexual contact—vaginal, anal or oral sex.
- Blood transfusions with contaminated blood.
- Injections with contaminated needles.

It is *not* contracted through:

- hugging or social kissing
- toilet seats
- mosquitoes
- swimming pools
- food
- eating utensils

People may be infected with HIV for as long as ten years before it develops into full-blown AIDS. During this period they may not even be aware of their condition. You cannot tell by looking at someone if they are infected as they will appear perfectly healthy.

The greatest chance travellers have of contracting HIV is through casual sexual encounters, particularly with prostitutes. In many countries you will be approached openly by prostitutes, but this group have a high incidence of HIV. It is claimed that all the prostitutes in Mombasa have HIV and it is thought that a large number of those in Bangkok are infected. Official figures should always be taken with a pinch of salt since some governments, such as Thailand, will deny the existence of AIDS in order to protect their revenue from sex-tourism.

The best way to avoid HIV infection is to steer clear of

prostitutes and casual sexual encounters: as yet there is no cure and a one-night stand could lead to a terminal illness.

If you do have casual sex, men should *always* wear a condom and women should insist that their male partners do so. Also, you should have a medical check-up and blood test soon afterwards—if you are infected with HIV you could pass it unknowingly to any sexual partners you have in the future.

The chances of becoming infected with HIV through contaminated blood are decreasing due to improved screening processes around the world, but it is still a potentially dangerous situation. However, if you are in the position where you need a blood transfusion it is unlikely you will be in a fit state to make enquiries about the quality of the blood which you are receiving. If you are travelling with other people, one of the group should insist that only blood that has been screened is used. It is also important to know your own blood group—you may be needed to give blood for someone with the same as yours.

Sterile supplies
One way to cut down on the possible risks of injections is to take a set of your own sterile needles, syringes and suturing (stitching) equipment. These can be bought from:

MASTA (as above)

British Airways Travel Clinic
   156 Regent Street
   London W1
   Tel: (0171) 439 9584 and throughout London

Safety and First Aid (SAFA)
   59 Hill Street
   Liverpool L8 5SA
   Tel: (0151) 708 0397

Travel Medical Centre Ltd
   Charlotte Keel Health Centre
   Seymour Road
   Easton
   Bristol BS5 0UA
   Tel: (0117) 935 4447

Make sure that these items are all clearly marked as First Aid and that you have a covering letter from your doctor stating why you are carrying them.

SNAKES AND SPIDERS

Snakes
As a rule snakes do not attack unless they feel challenged. Although only about 25 per cent of snakebites will be poisonous it is important to observe a few basic rules if someone is bitten by a snake:

1. DO NOT apply a tourniquet to the bite area.
2. Clean the infected area and cover it with a clean cloth.
3. Immobilise the limb with a splint.
4. DO NOT cut or suck the wound.
5. Give paracetamol but not asprin—this may cause bleeding from the stomach.
6. If the snake has been killed place it in a plastic bag to help the doctor administer the correct anti-venom.

One side-effect of a snakebite is that the victim may be suffering from shock.

Sea-snakes are one of the most poinonous varieties of snake but they usually only inhabit deep water. In northern Australia in the summer, beaches are provided with netted areas to allow swimmers protection from stingers (poisonous jellyfish) and occasionally sea-snakes.

Spiders
Many of the world's most poisonous spiders inhabit Australia, most notably the redback and the funnel-web. You can lower the risk of a spider (or scorpion) bite by:

● Shaking out shoes and boots first thing in the morning.
● Checking under toilet seats and around the rim of the toilet.
● Having reasonable protection around your ankles when walking in a spider-friendly environment.

If you are bitten by a spider there may be an anti-venom available, but you will have to get to a doctor fast.

SUGGESTED MEDICAL BAG

- Selection of plasters and bandages (including a continuous roll)
- Elasticated bandages of various sizes
- Paracetamol
- General anti-biotic—tetracycline
- Anti-malaria tablets
- Diarrhoea treatment—Imodium
- Rehydration sachets—Dioralyte, Rehydrat
- Anti-AIDS kit—needles, syringes, suturing material
- Condoms
- Travel sickness tablets—Dramamine, Phenergan
- Insect repellent—spray, gel, wipes or roll-on
- Insecticidal spray
- Anti-fungal cream—Canesten
- Anti-histamine cream
- Antiseptic cream
- Sun block
- Good quality sunglasses
- Water purification tablets
- Oil of cloves (for toothache)
- Multi-vitamins
- Dusting powder
- Indigestion tablets
- Throat lozenges
- Lip salve
- Cotton wool

All medical items should be packed in a clearly marked First Aid box.

TEN GOLDEN RULES FOR STAYING HEALTHY ABROAD

1. Get all relevant vaccinations before you go.
2. Take time to acclimatise properly.
3. Boil all drinking water and milk.
4. Do not eat uncooked or under-cooked meat or fish.
5. Avoid fly-infested restaurants if possible.
6. Do not have sex with prostitutes or inject drugs with contaminated needles.

7. Find out your anti-malarial requirements and take your pills as directed.
8. Wear several layers of loose-fitting clothing in cold climates—and avoid being in wet clothing for prolonged periods.
9. Only go swimming in bilharzia-free areas.
10. Have a full medical check-up when you return home.

11
Overcoming the Problems and Pitfalls of Travel

Some people have set off on a year abroad and had to return after only a few weeks because they have come across serious problems which they had not anticipated. However, forewarned is very much forearmed and if you know what to expect it will probably never happen.

MANAGING YOUR MONEY

Money seems to be a constant problem for most people and the traveller is no exception. What you will have to decide before you go is:

1. In what form do I want to take my money?
2. Do I want to leave some at home and have it sent out to me?
3. How do I want to carry it while I am travelling?
4. Do I want to take a credit card?
5. Do I have a back-up if I lose all my money?

If you intend being overseas for a year, particularly if a large part of that time will be taken up solely with travelling, you will need to take a substantial amount of money with you. This can be done in a number of forms:

- **Travellers cheques**. Thomas Cook and American Express travellers cheques are the most widely accepted around the world, with the latter being the best in terms of fast replacements if your cheques are stolen. You should get your cheques in a variety of small and large denominations—if you need money for your last day in a country whose currency is worthless outside its borders you do not want to have to cash a £50 travellers cheque. They should be in dollars or pounds

153

sterling and make sure you leave a list of the numbers with a
reliable contact at home. The safest way to carry large sums
of money while travelling.

- **Eurocheques**. Like a standard cheque book but not really
necessary if you have travellers cheques
- **Cash**. Every traveller should take some money in cash (approximately £100-200)—the American dollar is the most
widely accepted currency abroad. This can be used if you are
dealing in the black market (see below) or if you need to offer
bribes, since hard currency is much sought after. Again, a
variety of denominations are useful.
- **Credit cards**. These are not only the travellers' flexible friend
but sometimes their lifeline. If you have Visa and Access it is
a good idea to take both since some outlets worldwide only
take one or the other. An American Express card is also a
valuable asset—if you can afford one. The important thing
with credit cards is to use them for emergencies or the
occasional luxury, and not rely on them for everyday expenses.
If you do you will inevitably come across a country that has
very few outlets for any credit cards, such as Pakistan.

In order to pay off your credit cards you can leave some money
in your bank at home and have a standing order to pay a specific
sum each month or a direct debit to pay the whole amount due.
The former may be the best idea—if you have to unexpectedly pay
for an expensive item such as a flight there may not be enough in
the bank to cover the total amount. You can also credit your card
account before you go and this money will be taken off as you use
your card.

It is a good idea to spread your finances between different
methods. A suggested combination could be (for every £1000):
£600 in travellers cheques of different denominations; £100 in cash
(dollars and sterling); £300 left in a bank at home to pay off credit
card bills.

Another method of obtaining money is to leave a large lump sum
in your bank at home and have it wired to you at various
destinations abroad where the bank has a contact branch. Obviously, you need a bank that has contacts around the world
(Standard Chartered offer this type of service) but there are a
number of drawbacks with this method:

- It can be very expensive—bank charges of £60 for £500 transferred are not unheard of.
- It can be time consuming—you may have to wait several days in one place while the transfer is being completed.
- It can be unpredictable—not all banks around the world are computerised and telexes have been known to get lost and money to have gone missing.

How should I carry my money?

You should treat your money in the same way as your passport and carry it on your person at all times. This may lead to a bulky package in your money belt but this is preferable to having it in a pocket or backpack.

What if I become penniless?

If you do lose all your money, travellers cheques and credit cards you should resist the temptation to dig a large hole and jump into it. Report the loss or theft to the police, who will then give you confirmation which can be used when applying for replacement travellers cheques. If it is a genuine claim these will be issued in a day or two. Next, contact someone at home asking them to cancel your credit cards before a large international bill is run up at your expense. You could arrange for a new one to be sent to you but this is also fraught with risks. You should be able to get back most of your cash if it is covered by your insurance policy.

If you are completely penniless you could contact the nearest British Embassy. If you are lucky they may loan you some money but they will probably keep your passport as a guarantee that you will pay it back. This should be a last resort method.

Checklist

1. Have you spread your finances over a number of methods?
2. Have you left a list of your travellers cheque numbers with a contact at home?
3. Do you know where to go when abroad to claim replacement travellers cheques if necessary? (American Express and Thomas Cook issue booklets with the addresses of their overseas branches and outlets.)
4. Have you left sufficient money at home to pay off any credit card bills, and is it a standing order or direct debit?
5. Is there a family member or friend who could send you

emergency funds if you were destitute? (This can be done by telegraphic or mail transfer to bank overseas. It can take several days.)
6. Is your cash insured against theft or loss?
7. Have you a contingency plan if you lose all your money? (The important thing is to avoid having to come home.)

DEALING WITH THE BLACK MARKET

Black markets in foreign currency exist in less-developed countries around the world for two main reasons:

1. The governments set an unrealistically low exchange rate.
2. Locals want foreign currency (usually American dollars or pounds sterling) instead of local currency, which is useless outside their own country.

Some travellers believe it is morally wrong to contribute to the black market but these are greatly out-numbered by those who see it as an acceptable part of life abroad. Most travellers do change at least some of their money in this way and it is a two-way process: the locals are happy with their foreign currency and the traveller has more local currency to spend.

Currency declaration forms

To try and deter black-marketeers some governments, particularly in Africa and South America, insist that all travellers fill in a currency declaration form when they enter the country. This will state how much foreign currency you have, in travellers cheques and cash. Whenever you want to change money into local currency this transaction will be marked on your currency form. Ideally, when you leave the country the amount you have changed and the amount you have left should add up to the original total on your currency form.

Changing money on the black market

If you want to change money on the black market you will have to have some money that has not appeared on your currency declaration form. The easiest way to do this is to keep some aside from the amount you declare. The purist may argue that this is smuggling but as long as you are not greedy and keep it to reasonably small amounts then it may be overlooked by the authorities if they find it. This happened to one traveller as he was leaving Tanzania:

> 'As I was crossing the border the guards searched my baggage and found $25 that I had not declared. I thought I might be in for an extended stay in a Tanzanian jail but instead the guard just peeled off $5, gave me back the rest and smiled as I entered the country.'

How you choose to conceal the money is up to your own imagination but it is rare for body searches to take place. But be warned: some countries, including Ethiopia and Algeria, take currency forms very seriously.

Another way of getting around the question of the currency form is to change it before you cross a border. In some cases this will take considerable skill, while there are some countries where the currency form consists of a handwritten piece of paper.

The ethics of the black market
Many countries are lenient towards currency declaration forms and the black market: they know it goes on and as long as it does not get out of hand they turn a blind eye. In respect to this travellers should not abuse the system by trying to change all their money on the black market for the best price possible. Treat it as a privilege and don't be too greedy.

Exchange black market
Apart from money, goods such as clothing, electrical goods and records can be exchanged for large amounts of local currency in certain countries. This type of market is most common in Eastern Europe. In other parts of the world you may be offered a swap rather than cash.

What are the dangers of the black market?
Since the black market is illegal you have no one to turn to if you get ripped off, robbed or arrested. These things happen regularly (see below) but you can try and avoid it by:

- asking fellow travellers the best places to change money;
- never going up a side-street or alley alone;
- never displaying large amounts of foreign currency.

Do's and Don'ts of the black market

Do   — treat it with care and respect
         — have a good story if you get stopped at a border post
         — make sure someone seems reliable before changing
           money with them
         — ask the advice of other travellers

Don't   — be greedy
         — be careless
         — change large sums of money at one time
         — trust anyone completely.

HANDLING CONMEN

It is one of the unwritten laws of travel that where there are tourists
there will be people trying to con them out of their money and
belongings. As a rule there are two types:

● black market conmen
● all-purpose conmen

Black market conmen

Whenever anyone tries to change money on the black market they
run the risk of being conned. One of the favourite techniques is
for the conman to work with one or two accomplices who are, or
claim to be, policemen. Once you have changed your money you
will then be 'arrested' and forced to bribe your way out of trouble.
As with most other forms of business in these areas there is a certain
amount of haggling involved, as one unfortunate traveller found
in Kenya:

> 'After changing some money with a dealer on the black market I was
> arrested by a man who looked like a cross between Mike Tyson and
> Eddie Murphy. He told me that I would go to court in the morning
> and have to pay a fine of £600. He then offered me an alternative (there
> is usually an alternative)—if I paid him £60 he would let me go. By
> now I realised it was a scam but since I was technically in the wrong I
> eventually paid £20 for my release.'

Another favourite trick when changing money is for the conman
to show you an envelope with the money you are about to receive:
just as he gives it to you there is a commotion and the envelope

gets switched. When you look in the one you are given it contains nothing but newspaper.

All purpose conmen
These range from the ingenious to the mundane. These are some of the favourite cons:

The misplaced student
This will consist of one or two people coming up to you in the street and spinning a long and involved yarn about how they are students who have been forced to flee their own country because of persecution or war. Naturally, they are desperate to get back to see their families so could you, in the name of humanity, give them some money to help them get back home? Stories like this should be treated with a large fistful of salt and you should not hand over any money.

The shoe-shine boy
These occur throughout cities and towns in Third World countries. Some of them are kind, generous and helpful—and they give your shoes an excellent shine. Others are pernicious, spiteful and corrupt. Ignore shoe-shine boys who claim to be able to clean your training shoes with a special fluid—it is only water. More menacing are the shoe-shine boys who work in groups. You will agree a price with one of them before you start and by the time he has finished the price will have risen mysteriously. If you refuse to pay he will turn to his friends who will rally to his defence. You will then be faced by an angry group of shoe-shine boys. If you have the nerve you should pay the original price and walk away.

The dissident
In certain African countries there have been incidents where people have been approached by someone in a cafe. They will tell you they are a dissident and that they are being harassed by the police. They will not ask you for any money and you leave the cafe thinking that you have had an insight into the underside of the country. Once you are outside though you will be approached by two men who will say that you are under arrest for associating with a known dissident. You may then be taken to a room for interrogation. This is a very unnerving experience but it *is* a con and you should stick to your guns and not hand over any large amounts of money.

Eventually the conmen will get bored with your non-participation, but this may take several hours.

The corrupt policeman
This is a simple case of genuine policemen trying to make some extra money by intimidating travellers. They may stop you and ask you to turn out your pockets. If they find anything that they feel is incriminating (this may include an item such as a Swiss Army knife) they will try to make you pay an instant fine. If you ask to see their superior they will soon get cold feet.

The Youth Hostel bus
Be wary of people who pick you up at an airport and offer you a ride to the Youth Hostel, or a cheap hotel, with their 'courtesy' bus. The chances are that it will appear to run out of petrol almost immediately and the driver will ask you to lend him some money for petrol (it will probably be an inordinately large amount of money for the quantity of fuel involved). He will then drop you at your destination, promise to come back with your money—and disappear into the sunset.

The currency form con
Some conmen recognise the value of the currency declaration form to the traveller and go to extreme lengths to get them to part with it. This may range from a simple offer to change money for you at a highly lucrative rate, to an involved plan about buying an expensive piece of electrical equipment, which can only be done with the use of your form. If you do hand over your form, the next time you see your new-found friend he will be in the company of the obligatory phoney policemen. Since they have a document which you need when you leave the country you can expect to do some fairly hard bargaining.

The street-seller
The sale of 'genuine' artefacts around the world is one that is open to wide-scale abuse. Unless you are an expert in the field you will be unable to tell a Ming vase from a ceramic dish made a week ago. One way around this is to enlist the help of a local when buying these artefacts. Alternatively, accept the fact that you may have been conned and hope nobody ever tells you.

How do I deal with conmen?

There is a fine line between openness and gullibility as far as travellers and conmen are concerned. The tricksters will invariably appear very friendly and genuine and may spend hours with you to win your confidence before they make their move. They may even buy you drinks and cups of tea to demonstrate their generosity.

As a rule you should be wary of people who seem over-eager to impress you. A certain amount of cynicism is needed when people first approach you. While you do not want to scare off someone who is genuinely interested in helping you, you should take things slowly—if they are genuine they will respect this and a friendship may develop. If they are conmen they may tire quickly of your wariness and move on to a more unsuspecting victim. Other points to consider are:

- Never give someone important documents such as currency forms or passports—this is a ticket to bribery.

- If you are 'arrested' by the accomplices of a conman insist to be taken to the police station. Even if they are genuine policemen they will be very reluctant to do this and may prefer to let you go.

- If you lend anyone some money make sure you stay with them until you get it back.

- Always see what you are getting before you pay for it—do not give someone money to buy an item for you.

- Trust your instincts—if something does not feel right then move on.

- Be bold—conmen can be very pushy and if you are as challenging in return they may back down. This does not mean you should get physical, but rather ask them questions that may unease them.

COPING WITH THEFT

This is one of the most unpleasant experiences abroad and one that takes several forms:

- pickpockets
- distractors
- sneak-thieves
- snatchers
- violent theft

Pickpockets

Even if you are pickpocketed this should not cause a great deal of trauma if you have all your valuables in a money belt. You may lose some loose change but this is not the end of the world. But it underlines the importance of not putting any valuables in pockets.

Pickpockets tend to operate where there are crowds: main streets, local bus stations and sporting events. Be particularly careful in these areas.

Distractors

These are thieves who steal from you while you are concentrating on a diversion, which take several forms. These are some examples from around the world:

- In Brazil, travellers have had a powerful itching agent put down their backs. As they have been scrambling out of their clothes the thieves have ransacked their discarded bags. This is a popular method for stealing cameras.

- In France, travellers have been accosted by groups of children flapping large pieces of cardboard in their faces. As they try to fend them off their pockets are picked.

- In the former Yugoslavia, a woman with a baby in her arms approaches unsuspecting travellers. Suddenly, the baby is thrown to the startled visitor. While he catches the infant and recovers his composure his pockets and bag are plundered. The 'baby' turns out to be a doll.

- In a bus station in Zimbabwe fights have been organised for the benefit of travellers. As they crowd around to see what is happening a number of people set to work on their belongings.

It is hard to recommend a general defence for every instance of this kind which you might come across. The most important thing is to be aware of the dangers and try to recover your composure as quickly as possible if you are subjected to a diversion attack.

Sneak-thieves
Again, these come in all varieties: on local transport, in hotels, even people who have used knives to slit tents and sleeping bags while people are asleep in them. Some places are more prone to this type of theft than others—beach huts in Thailand, for example, are a popular target but the golden rule is:

- Don't leave valuables lying around unattended.

For the times you are asleep it is worth taking a few padlocks so you can lock hotel rooms from inside. Also be careful of the windows: thieves will go to incredible lengths, and heights, to get to your valuables.

Snatchers
The most common example of this is moped drivers in Italy, who drive past tourists, swiping their handbags or daypacks as they go. There are also the unmotorised snatchers who operate on foot. You can minimise the risks of this by:

1. Wearing your daypack around your chest—like a joey in a kangaroo's pouch.
2. Strengthening the belts of moneybelts with thin wire such as piano wire. You should be wary of this if you have a neck-wallet—you do not want to save your money at the expense of your head.

Violent theft
Thankfully this is not as common as the media would like to make out and it should be remembered that it is only the bad news that makes the headlines: there is not much mileage in announcing, 'Thousands of people travelled all over the world today without incident'. Having said that it does occur and prevention is better than the cure:

- Don't walk along unlit streets, parks or beaches at night.
- Don't flaunt expensive equipment such as cameras.
- Always look positive and if you are lost don't appear too

helpless—thieves usually pick on the weakest looking
travellers.
● Try to talk your way out of awkward situations rather than
resorting to physical violence.

If you are confronted by someone with a gun or a knife, give
them what they want. This does not mean you should hand over
your entire belongings. They will probably be most interested in
cash so give them this first. If they then ask for your passport and
travellers cheques then hand them over too—all these things can
be replaced, you cannot.

JUST YOUR CREDIT CARDS. I DON'T
FEEL SAFE CARRYING CASH ROUND HERE!

WOMEN TRAVELLERS

Even in these liberated days it can be considerably more difficult
for female travellers than their male counterparts. In many Third
World countries men and women have to travel separately and in
Tanzania a station master was appalled when one female voyager
wanted to travel in the same compartment as her boyfriend.

Muslim countries can be notoriously difficult for women
travellers and you have to realise that many countries will have
different moral codes to our own. If you want to ward off unwanted
advances you should:

● dress conservatively;
● wear sunglasses to prevent eye-contact;
● learn some stern rubukes in the local language.

For further information concerning women travellers consult:

Women Travel (Rough Guide)
Handbook for Women Travellers (Piatkus).

CHECKLIST FOR SAFETY ABROAD

1. Keep your money in your money-belt at all times.
2. Research the workings of the black market currency exchange before taking the plunge.
3. Always be on your guard in crowded areas.
4. Never trust anyone immediately.
5. If you are arrested stick to your guns if you know you are in the right.
6. If you feel uneasy anywhere get out quickly.
7. Never part with any important documents.
8. Always try to look confident.
9. Try not to look too affluent.
10. If you are a woman be prepared to be faced by an unfair world.

12
Coming Home

One of the hardest aspects of a year abroad is adjusting to life at home when you return. The concept of culture shock is often mentioned in relation to visiting different countries, but after a year of weird, wayout and wonderful experiences abroad it can be even more of a shock to come back to the everyday realities of life at home. The first thing you will notice is how similar everything seems in comparison to what you have done with your year.

READJUSTING

When you get home you should take a few steps to overcome your 'returning home shock'. You can do this by:

1. Putting things in perspective. It can be very depressing to come home and either return to the same old way of life or, worse, face the prospect of unemployment and an uncertain future. But if you look at these situations in terms of what you have done with your year abroad then they will not look so bleak. It can be very comforting to know that you have done something unique: with this knowledge it is a lot easier to confront any uncertainties that face you in the future.

2. Preserving what you have done. The memory of even the most exhilarating experiences fade with time so when you get home you should produce a concrete record of your time abroad:

- Put your photographs in an album rather than letting them gather dust in a drawer.
- Transfer your photographs onto a video tape.
- If you kept a diary then write this up and add your thoughts

once you have the chance to look at the experience with hindsight.

- Produce an overall project of your year abroad—this will not only delight family and friends but it will also bring a glazed look to your eyes when you read it in years to come.
- Try writing articles for newspapers or magazines (see Chapter Five).
- Keep in touch with people you met during your time abroad—having visitors from overseas is one of the best ways to relive your own experiences.

3. Looking to the future. If after a period of time (at least two or three months) you still feel unsettled then you should think seriously about spending another year abroad. One year often expands to two or three and you should not feel guilty if this is what you really want to do. After spending a year abroad between school and university students frequently repeat the exercise once they have graduated. Some even make a full-time career of it.

RETURNING TO THE JOB MARKET

This is one of the vast grey areas after spending a year abroad. Personnel officers generally say they are in favour of people who have spent a year abroad, citing benefits such as personal growth and greater experiences. However, this enthusiasm is generally confined to:

- School-leavers who have spent an organised year abroad after school.
- Graduates who have spent *one* year abroad after university.

Although they will admire your adventurous spirit they are not so keen on:

- Graduates who have spent more than one year abroad.
- People who give up a career and take a year abroad in mid-life.

With increasing unemployment, (particularly graduate un-employment which, according to the Association of Graduate Careers Advisory Services' Central Services Unit, is approaching the ten per cent mark), people contemplating a year abroad will have to consider how it will effect their employment prospects once they return.

There is one school of thought that argues it is not worth working for an employer who does not recognise the benefits of a year abroad. If people have the confidence to spend a year abroad then they will probably have the ability to find a good job when they return. The public sector are very open-minded when it comes to employing people who have spent a year abroad.

How do I show my experiences in the best possible way?

When trying to re-enter the job market you should be proud of your experiences and show them in the best possible light. Instead of writing on your CV 'I spent six months in Peru working with local tribes', say 'I spent six months organising the local tribes in the construction of a new irrigation system. I was in charge of a group of ten people, which involved management skills, inter-personal skills, flexibility, initiative and stamina. The system was completed on time and has doubled the village's agricultural output.' Do not be afraid to sell yourself:

- Explain what you did, with the emphasis on the positive contributions you made.
- State what you learnt from the experience.
- Show how you have benefited personally.
- Discuss the benefits that you will be able to bring your employer.

Alternative employment

If you do not want to go back on the treadmill of conventional employment you could consider alternative means of earning a living. This could be anything from an independent travel consultant to setting up your own voluntary organisation. People have even been known to write books based on their experiences abroad.

A PERSONAL ACCOUNT

James Neilson, from Edinburgh, spent 18 months abroad after graduating with a degree in business management:

'When I graduated I felt there was too much to see and do in the world to be stuck in one career for the rest of my life, so I decided to go overseas for a year.

'Planning the year was one of the most important parts: I wrote to the embassies of all the countries I hoped to visit, to find out about entry and health requirements. The one thing that became clear from this is that most countries state that you should have an onward ticket at the time of entry. In reality though there was never any hassle with this: a smart set of clothes (even at border crossings in the middle of the bush) and a reasonable amount of money always ensured that the onward ticket was never an issue.

'I chose to split the year into two: for the first six months I travelled overland through Africa and Asia and then I spent the next year working in Australia on a Holiday Working Visa.

'My experiences in Africa and Asia were incredible and it is something that will stay with me for the rest of my life. Everyday there was something new to learn and see and I realised very quickly what a small part of the world Britain is. Travelling on public transport proved to be not only very cheap but an ideal way to meet people—I think they respect travellers who are mad enough to get on the local buses! People have since asked me what my favourite country was but it would be unfair to single out any one place—everywhere had something to offer.

'Once I reached Australia I started in north Queensland and worked my way down the coast. I spent some time working as a dishwasher and then as a barman in Brisbane. I then went to Victoria to pick grapes for a few weeks. This was enlightening to say the least—by and large the growers only want to get their fruit picked and they do not care how this is achieved. It is not an environment for the faint-hearted or those looking for a quiet life. When I was not working I drove across the Nullabor desert to Perth. This was fun for the first twelve hours but after three days of looking at nothing but desert scrub I was glad to reach the west coast.

'Since I have returned home I have set up my own business. Although it is a reasonably stressful job I hope that my experiences abroad have made me more patient and able to handle the pressures. If I could do it all again—I would do it all again.'

**QUESTIONS TO ASK YOURSELF WHEN YOU
RETURN**

1. Am I happy with what I have done?
2. Am I happy with being back home?
3. Have I spent enough time getting used to being back home?
4. Do I want to spend another year abroad?
5. If so, what do I want to do?
6. Do I have a good record of what I have done?
7. Can I show employers that I have benefited from a year abroad?
8. Have I learnt things that could lead to a new career?
9. Can I pass on my experiences to others?
10. Will life ever be the same again?

Useful Addresses

GENERAL

British Universities North America Club (BUNAC), 16 Bowling Green Lane, London EC1R 0BD. Tel: (0171) 251 3472.

Camp America, 37a Queen's Gate, London SW7 5HR. Tel: (0171) 581 7373.

Careers Research and Advisory Centre (CRAC), Bateman Street, Cambridge CB2 1LZ. Tel: (01223) 460277

Central Bureau for Educational Visits and Exchanges, 10 Spring Gardens, London SW1A 2BN. Tel: (0171) 389 4004. A wealth of information and literature covering a wide range of opportunities for working and studying abroad.

Concordia Youth Service Volunteers, 8 Brunswick Place, Hove, East Sussex BN3 1ET. Tel: (01273) 772086.

GAP Activity Projects, 44 Queen's Road, Reading, Berks RG1 4BB. Tel: (0118) 959 4914.

How To Books Ltd, Plymbridge House, Estover Road, Plymouth PL6 7PZ. Tel: (01752) 695745. Fax: (01752) 695699.

Intercultural Educational Programme (IEP), 33 Seymour Place, London W1H 5AP. Tel: (0171) 402 3305.

International Voluntary Service (IVS), Old Hall, East Bergholt, Colchester CO7 6TQ. Tel: (01206) 298215.

Kibbutz Representatives, 1A Accommodation Road, London NW11. Tel: (0181) 458 9235.

Project Trust, The Hebridean Centre, Isle of Coll, Argyll PA78 6TE. Tel: (01879) 230 444.

Trailfinders, 42–50 Earls Court Road, London W8 6FT. Tel: (0171) 938 3366.

Vacation Work, 9 Park End Street, Oxford OX1 1HJ. Tel: (01865) 241978.

Voluntary Service Overseas (VSO), 317 Putney Bridge Road, London SW15 2PN. Tel: (0181) 780 2266.

Volunteer Centre, 29 Lower King's Road, Berkhamsted, Herts HP4 2AE.

WEXAS International Ltd, 45–49 Brompton Road, London SW3 1DE. Tel: (0171) 589 0500.

Youth Hostel Association, Trevelyan House, 8 St Stephen's Hill, St Albans, Herts AL1 2DY. Tel: (01727) 55215.

HEALTH

British Airways Immunisation Centre, 156 Regent Street, London W1. Tel: (0171) 439 9584.

Department of Infections and Tropical Medicine, East Birmingham Hospital, Bordesley Green East, Birmingham B9 5ST. Tel: (0121) 766 6611.

Hospital for Tropical Diseases, 4 St Pancras Way, London NW1 0PE. Tel: (0171) 388 9600 (travel clinic) or (0839) 337733 (pre-recorded healthline).

Department of Infection and Tropical Medicine, Ruchill Hospital, Glasgow G20 9NB. Tel: (0141) 946 7120.

Further Reading

WORK

Applying for a United States Visa, Richard Fleischer (How To Books)
How to Find Temporary Work Abroad, Nick Vandome (How To Books)
How to Get a Job Abroad, Roger Jones (How To Books)
How to Get a Job In America, Roger Jones (How To Books)
How to Get a Job in Australia, Nick Vandome (How To Books)
How to Get a Job in Europe, Mark Hempshell (How To Books)
How to Get a Job in France, Mark Hempshell (How To Books)
How to Get a Job in Germany, Christine Hall (How To Books)
How to Live & Work in America, Roger Jones (How To Books)
How to Live & Work in Australia, Laura Veltman (How To Books)
How to Live & Work in Germany, Christine Hall (How To Books)
How to Get a Job in Hotels & Catering, M. Hempshell (How To Books)
How to Get a Job in Travel & Tourism, M. Hempshell (How To Books)
How to Travel Round the World, Nick Vandome (How to Books)
Living & Working in France, Nicole Prevost Logan (How To Books)
Working Abroad—The Daily Telegraph Guide to Working and Living Overseas (Kogan Page, 120 Pentonville Road, London N1 9JN)
Working in Japan, Jonathan Hayter (How To Books)
Working in the European Communities (CRAC)
Directory of Jobs and Careers Abroad (Vacation Work)
Work Your Way Around the World (Vacation Work)
Working Holidays (Central Bureau)
Directory of Work and Study in Developing Countries (Vacation Work)
Summer Jobs Abroad (Vacation Work)
Working in Europe (Department of Employment—free)
The Au Pair and Nanny's Guide to Working Abroad (Vacation Work)
How to Teach Abroad, Roger Jones (How To Books)
Jobs in Japan (Vacation Work)
Kibbutz Volunteer (Vacation Work)

STUDY

How to Study Abroad, Teresa Tinsley (How To Books)
How to Master Languages, Roger Jones (How To Books)
Higher Education in the European Community (HMSO, PO Box 276, London Sw8 5DT)
Scholarships Abroad (British Council). Mainly postgraduates.
Scholarships for International Students (CRAC). For students wishing to study in the USA.
The Student Handbook (Macmillan Publishers Ltd, 4 Little Essex Street, London WC2R 3LF)
Home from Home (Central Bureau)
Study Abroad. International Scholarships, International Courses (HMSO)
Study Holidays (Central Bureau)

VOLUNTARY WORK

Volunteer Work (Central Bureau)
International Directory of Voluntary Work (Vacation Work)
How to Do Voluntary Work Abroad (How To Books)

TRAVEL

The Traveller's Handbook (WEXAS)
The Budget Travel Handbook (Horizon, Plymbridge House, Estover Road, Plymouth PL6 7PZ)
An Explorer's Handbook (Hodder & Stoughton, 47 Bedford Square, London WC1B 3DP)
Women Travel (Rough Guide, Harrap Columbus, Chelsea House, 26 Market Square, Bromley, Kent BR1 1NA)
Handbook for Women Travellers (Piatkus, 5 Windmill Street, London W1P 1HF)
Nothing Ventured—Disabled People Travel the World (Rough Guide)
Overseas Timetable—Railway, Road and Shipping (Thomas Cook)
Lonely Planet Guides PO Box 617, Hawthorn, Victoria 3122, Australia
Rough Guides

HEALTH

Traveller's Health: How to Stay Healthy Abroad (OUP, Walton Street, Oxford OX2 6DP)
The Traveller's Health Guide (Lascelles, 47 York Road, Brentford, Middlesex TW8 0QP)

Index